JANN JOHNSON'S DISCOVERY BOOK OF CRAFTS

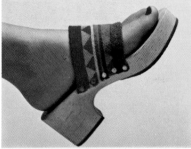

Book Design by Jay Peterson

Photographs by Gary D. Johnson

Illustrations by Kathy De Wein and Joyce Culkin

JANN JOHNSON'S DISCOVERY BOOK OF CRAFTS

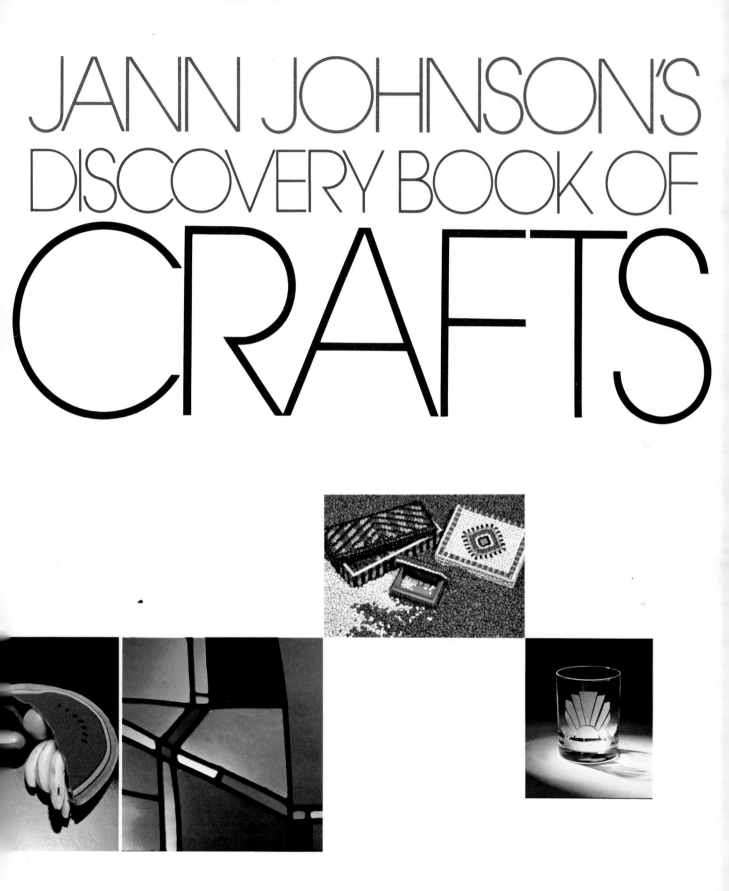

Reader's Digest Press · New York · 1975

Distributed by E. P. DUTTON & CO., INC.

TO THE MEMORY
OF MY LOVING GRANDMOTHER,
SWEET NELL MC BETH

ACKNOWLEDGMENTS

This book represents the work of a large number of generous and enthusiastic people. I sincerely appreciate their interest and efforts and wish to express an enormous thank you to:

Barbara Anderson, whose initiative launched the project; Albert Leventhal, whose confidence, patience and humor never failed, even in times of stress; Regina Grant Hersey, who perseveringly unscrambled my manuscript and transformed it; Gary Johnson, my brother, an excellent photographer and craftsman whose work appears on these pages; Jay Peterson, an award-winning graphic and package designer, who used his designing talents in the layout of this book; Kathy De Wein and Joyce Culkin, whose illustrations appear on these pages; Kathy Duffy, who dedicated her artistic skills and numerous hours to many of the projects; all my friends who helped with the projects—Leta Richmond, Andrea Ungar, Cathy Higgins, Carol Nicklaus, David O'Grady, Beth Blumenthal, Eric Camiel, Carla Guiffreda, Ron Kuriloff, Lois Steinhardt, Richie Blumenthal, Ann Benedetto, Cecilia Waters, Jane Quinson, Margo Appleton, Aune Merikallio at Best Foods and the many other friends who made patchwork squares for the Friendship Quilt; the models, Beverly Johnson, Cathy Higgins, Mary Randolph Carter Berg, Teresa Morgan, Bill Blumenthal, Tom Richmond and Sanda Ungar; Chuck La Monica and Ken Tannenbaum, who let us use their studios for photography; Leonore Fleischer, who started me on my writing career with *The Jeans Book*; and to *Reader's Digest* for having the great taste to publish my book!

J.J.

Published by
READER'S DIGEST PRESS · NEW YORK

An original work produced by
Vineyard Books, Inc.
159 East 64th Street
New York, New York 10021

Published simultaneously in Canada by Clarke, Irwin & Company, Limited, Toronto and Vancouver.

ISBN: 0-88349-045-5

Printed in Hong Kong by Mandarin Publishers Limited.

CONTENTS

HOW TO USE THIS BOOK

Before beginning any of the projects, familiarize yourself with the information in the back of the book—the sections on materials, methods for enlarging and reducing, glossaries for needlepoint, knitting, crocheting and embroidery. Note in particular the section titled *Sources for Materials*. This list of resources is keyed with numbers that correspond to the numbers following certain unusual items in the Materials sections of various projects and indicates where those items may be purchased.

When you have selected a project to make, read the instructions and study the photograph, figures and patterns to get a clear idea of how to proceed. Now is the time to decide on any changes or alterations you wish to make. Assemble all your materials before you begin. Nothing is more frustrating than to find a crucial ingredient missing when you are in the middle of a project. (It is a good idea to organize in a box or other container the tools and materials you will use frequently. Always clean your tools and brushes before storing them.)

Work step by step, following the instructions as carefully as you can. You will find that even the more challenging projects go smoothly when you do exactly what the instructions tell you to do.

When you have completed a project it is a good idea to make note of any changes or substitutions you have made, the time the project took to complete, the amount of money you spent for materials and any other information you wish to record for future reference.

COUNTRY SOAP

Simple, wholesome Country Soap is almost as down to earth and basic as home-made bread. It has a natural, pleasant odor, the good looks and unusual character of something hand-made and has pure, quality ingredients and no chemical fillers. Country Soap is gentle, luxurious and pampers your skin with natural glycerin, often removed from commercial soaps.

The following formula has been tested by Kathy and me. I must warn you that making soap can be messy and that the lye must be handled with caution. Should lye come in contact with the skin, rinse the affected area immediately with cool running water. Keep children away from the working area and store unused ingredients where children cannot reach them. If you follow the directions carefully you should be successful on your first try. Good luck!

MATERIALS

newspaper

5-lb. scale[18] that measures in half ounces (it will also come in handy for cooking, especially for diets)

rubber gloves

apron

a sturdy quart jar with tight-fitting lid or a large measuring cup

ice pick or hammer and nail

pot holders

2 large wooden spoons

2 meat thermometers with a range of at least 90°–140° in 5° gradations (aluminum is O.K.)

large pan of cold water

enameled 3-qt. pan

milk carton—clean, empty quart size—or small box of like size (with plastic liner)

heavy blanket

FORMULA

10 oz. water

3⅓ oz. lye[21]

14 oz. pure unsalted olive oil

6 oz. coconut oil, from a health-food store

7½ oz. white solid vegetable shortening

1 heaping tablespoon uncooked regular oatmeal

1 heaping tablespoon honey (optional)

a few drops of oil-based scent[9] (optional)

METHOD
Step 1
Assemble formula ingredients and materials on newspaper-covered working area.

Step 2
If you are using a glass jar with tight-fitting lid (which I recommend), punch two holes in the lid at opposite edges (see fig. 1).

Step 3
We will be measuring by the "weighing by addition" method. It's quick, accurate and helps make your soap turn out right every time. Make the lye solution first, being sure to wear rubber gloves and to rinse immediately in cool running water anything that comes in contact with the lye. Place the jar (or cup) on the scale and write down its weight. Slowly add water to the jar until the scale reads 10 ounces more than the weight of the empty jar. Write down the weight again. Cautiously add the lye, averting your face from the fumes, until the scale reads 3⅓ ounces more than the last weight noted. The lye solution will be very hot (180°–220°), so handle with care. Remove jar from scale with pot holders and stir with wooden spoon until all the lye is dissolved. (It will change color only slightly.) Set the lye solution in a pan of cold water and cool until the thermometer registers 97°.

Step 4
Measure the oils and shortening into the enamel pan, using the weighing-by-addition method. Remember that this measurement is different from measurement by the fluid ounce. The formula won't work if you measure it in cups and tablespoons. (I tried it.) When the oils are measured, heat to melt the shortening and then cool to 97°. (I suggest using two thermometers, one for the lye solution and one for the oils.)

Step 5
When both the lye solution and the oils are exactly at 97° you are ready to introduce the lye solution into the oils. Cap the jar with the lye solution, stir the oils with a wooden spoon and, while stirring smoothly, pour the lye solution through one of the holes in the cap or in a thin stream from the cup (see fig. 2). The mixture will start to thicken slightly and turn opaque. This is called *saponification*. After 10 to 30 minutes of vigorous stirring you should be able to drop some of the mixture from the spoon and see it stand out momentarily from the rest of the mixture (see fig. 3). If this doesn't happen, keep on stirring. Sometimes it can take as long as an hour.

Step 6

It is now time to add the oatmeal to the mixture, along with the honey and scent, if you wish. Mix thoroughly and quickly pour into the milk carton. Cover immediately with the blanket to keep the mixture warm (see fig. 4), for cold air can sometimes inhibit the chemical reaction.

Step 7

Within 24 hours you should have solid soap. Remove the soap by sliding it out of the carton or box. Though you'll be tempted to use it right away, don't. It needs to age and breathe, and there is a chemical reaction still going on.

Step 8

After two to four weeks your soap will be ready for shaping and carving. Trim off the hard outside edges first, for these can be drying to the skin. You can cut off plain slices, cut out shapes with cookie cutters, make tiny guest bars or small bars for travel. Or carve a design or initial. Make a huge shower ball by shaping the soap securely around the loose ends of a loop of soft thick cotton cable. (If you make a shower ball, give it plenty of time to harden, for the soap will still be soft.)

VARIATIONS

You can make a double recipe and carve one half as a Country Soap loaf tied with gingham to use a slice at a time. Rub the top with cocoa to give it a "crust". (And you'll have enough scraps left over to make soap balls.)

If you wish to color the soap, use candle coloring, melted wax crayons or cocoa sparingly. Color is always added after saponification.

Experiment with additions such as Vitamin E or almond meal instead of oatmeal. A big spoonful of olive oil added after saponification enriches the soap and is great for dry skin.

Do not add fruit. It will turn to mush and ruin the soap. If you want to make strawberry soap, for example, tint the formula pink (lipstick works, believe it or not) and add some strawberry oil essence. *Remember that all additions are made after saponification.* I hope that you enjoy making Country Soap as much as I do!

Fig. 1

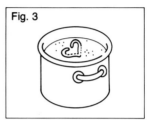

Fig. 2

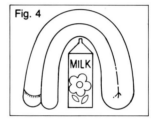

Fig. 3

Fig. 4

MILK

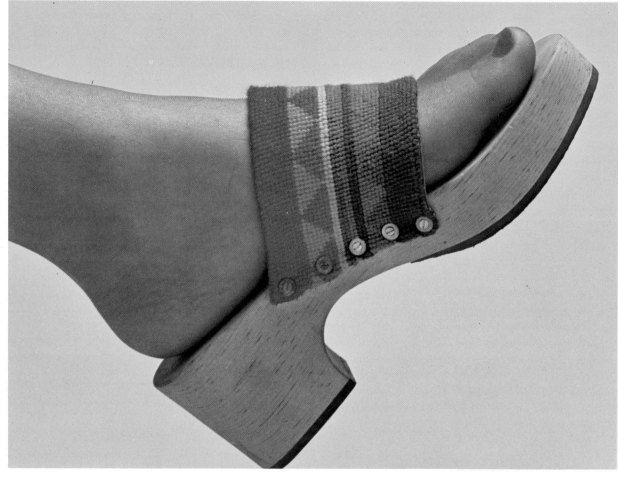

CLOGS

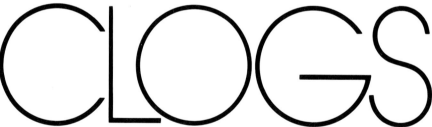

A small project in needlepoint is especially reward-ing because it takes only a short time to complete. This project is so much the better because you can display (and enjoy) your handiwork every time you wear your clogs. They look great with jeans, pants and on the beach. The needlepoint pieces are small enough to fit into your handbag for those extra moments when you can do a few stitches. I gave this project to Barbara, an incredibly busy friend, and her enthusiasm was gratifying; she finished the needlework in two evenings. The wooden clog bot-toms may be found in hobby shops, or, if you wish, you may take apart a pair of wooden-bottomed shoes by removing the screws.

MATERIALS

needlepoint canvas—13 squares to the inch, large enough for two patterns or about 12″ square[1]

permanent felt-tip markers

1 skein of needlepoint yarn in each of the following colors: red, magenta, orange, yellow, bright green, turquoise, purple[1]

contact cement

1 pair wooden clog bottoms[5]

sandpaper

screwdriver

two dozen ½″ brass screws and ⅛″ washers[21]

pencil

METHOD

Step 1

The needlepoint uppers (as they are called in shoe biz) are made on a straight piece of canvas, 13 squares to the inch. The pattern I give on page 160 is only a guide. There are many factors that may alter the pattern—the number of squares per inch on the canvas, the heaviness of the yarn you use, the type of backing and the kind of wooden bottom. Trace the pattern on two pieces of canvas with a light-colored permanent marker. (Never use a pencil, because pencil marks can bleed during blocking.)

Step 2

Fold under ½″ seam allowance of lengthwise edges along a thread of the canvas. You will stitch through this double thickness, creating finished edges. Use the basic needlepoint stitch (see fig. 1) and do the following: nine rows of red, seven rows of interlocking triangles in magenta and orange, two rows of yellow, two rows of green, two rows of turquoise, two rows of purple, seven rows of interlocking triangles in turquoise and green and nine rows of purple to finish.

Step 3

Periodically while doing the needlepoint, stand on the wooden bottom and place the partially stitched canvas across the arch of the foot, clearing toes. Use the photograph as a guide. Make sure that the uppers overlap the sides of the clogs at least ½″ to ¾″ so that they can be attached to the clogs with screws. Keep in mind that the backing for the uppers will take up some of the width.

Step 4

When the uppers are finished, block them by dipping them in warm water and stretching back to the original shape. Place face down on a towel and press. Carefully take out any stitches that were folded under. If you don't, the uppers will look lumpy.

Step 5

Trim raw edges to ⅝″ from stitching.

Step 6

Back the uppers with natural-colored leather or sturdy fabric. Don't be tempted to use a bright-colored leather, for the color might come off on your feet. Glue the backing to the needlepoint, neatly turning the canvas edges under and out of sight. The leather can be trimmed later. Use a glue that will remain flexible; contact cement works well.

Step 7

Allow the uppers to dry in a rounded shape similar to your feet to prevent buckling when attached to the bottom (see fig. 2). A row of machine stitches near the edges will help keep the backing and the uppers together. Trim leather if necessary. Dot edges of canvas with matching permanent marker so that leather doesn't show.

Step 8

Sand the wooden bottoms until smooth.

Step 9

Stand on the wooden bottoms, place the uppers across your insteps and have a friend mark the edges lightly on the sides of the clog with a pencil (see fig. 3).

Step 10

Put screws with washers directly through the needlepoint into the wood (about five to a side). I advise putting a few crucial screws halfway in, checking and correcting the fit and then screwing in securely. The uppers can be unscrewed for dry cleaning.

VARIATIONS

You might want to make another pair of uppers in earth tones, such as rust, black, cream, chocolate, tan, raw umber and ivory. They'd look great with all the natural cottons.

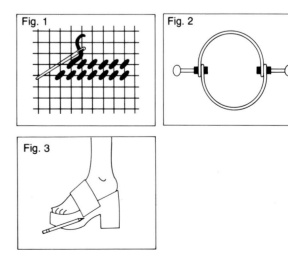

Fig. 1

Fig. 2

Fig. 3

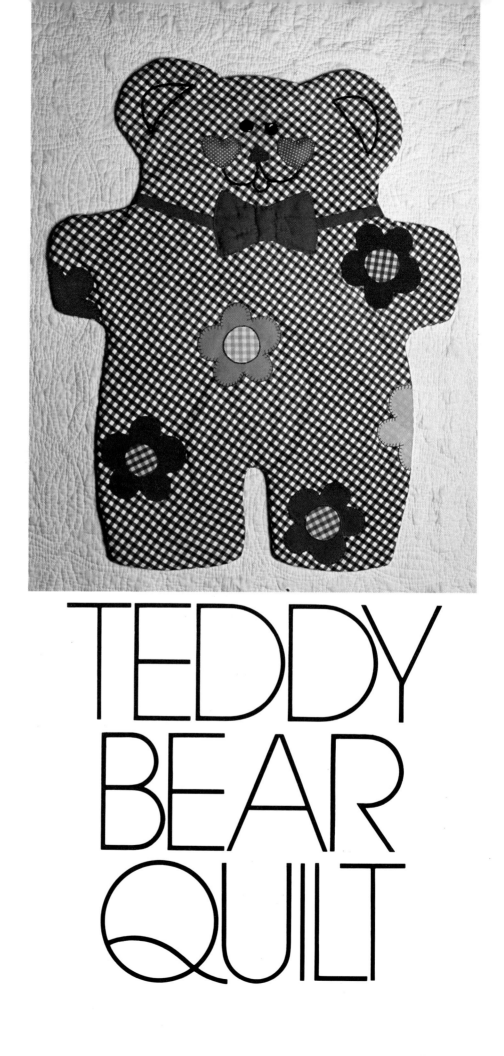

TEDDY BEAR QUILT

Every baby loves a teddy bear. Here is a new version of the most-loved toy, a Teddy-Bear Quilt. The quilt shown here was made for Carter. It has become such a favorite of his that I had a hard time borrowing it from him to take the picture. The quilt is decorative, practical and delightful, according to Carter.

MATERIALS

tracing paper

pencil or tailor's chalk

stiff paper (tag board or cardboard) for pattern

2 yds. brown gingham, colorfast, preshrunk

straight pins

⅛ yd. each red, yellow, orange, green and blue gingham and ⅛ yd. solid-color cotton in each of the above colors (to match), colorfast, preshrunk

pink and white dotted cotton for cheeks (the smallest piece you can buy), colorfast, preshrunk

iron-on bonding tape (found in most dime stores)

sewing machine

iron

1 pkg. rolled quilt filling[17]

1 spool red thread

red embroidery thread for hand embroidery (optional)

1 spool brown thread (matching the brown gingham)

2 black buttons for eyes

METHOD

Step 1

Using the method on page 150, enlarge the pattern on page 161 and trace to stiff paper.

Step 2

Trace patterns for flowers, bow tie, cheeks and nose onto stiff paper.

Step 3

Place the body pattern piece on the bias of the brown gingham and mark two side by side in pencil or tailor's chalk. Cut out and mark design for ears and mouth and eye placement with a pencil or chalk.

Step 4

Decide how many flowers you want and cut from the solid-color fabric with centers cut from the matching gingham.

Step 5

Cut neck band and bow tie from the solid-blue fabric, the cheeks from the pink and white and the nose from red.

Step 6

Pin nose, cheeks, flowers, tie and neck band on one of the body pieces, using the photograph as a guide.

Step 7

Cut bonding tape in ⅛" strips, slip under the edges of all appliqué edges and press for ten seconds with the tip of a medium-hot iron. This step makes the zigzag sewing a snap.

Step 8

Pin the flower "tail" and the back neck band on the other body piece and follow the instructions in step 7.

Step 9

Roll out quilt filling, pin on wrong side of the teddy-bear front, cut and baste edges.

Step 10

Using a sewing machine set for a close zigzag stitch, sew around all appliqué edges in red. The stitch should resemble the embroidery satin stitch. (Practice the stitch on a scrap of material to get it just right.) Using the brown thread, zigzag ears and mouth, following the pencil or chalk lines. *Securely* sew on buttons for eyes (babies like to pull at them).

Step 11

With right sides together, baste edges of body together. Machine-stitch, leaving a ½" seam allowance and a 4" opening on one side. Take out basting stitches, trim seam allowance to ¼" and press. Turn right side out, press again (pressing the raw edge of the opening under ¼") and slipstitch the opening closed. You now have a machine-washable quilt that any baby would be proud to love.

VARIATIONS

The appliqués may be hand-embroidered with a blanket stitch, for example. This is very effective, though it does take longer than zigzagging by machine.

You can make a wall hanging by stitching the finished bear to another piece of material, or try your hand at making other animals, such as ducks or hippos, making sure that the shapes are pudgy and appealing. Just think what a great baby-shower present you now can give.

PLACEMAT PURSES

A natural straw handbag is an indispensable summer accessory. The bags described in the following project are made from place mats. You can use rectangular mats, or round and oval ones (for a shoulder bag). Pick mats that have neat edges; they will give your bag a more finished look. These purses are perfect for gift-giving or for just spoiling yourself with a whole collection of inexpensive but pretty bags.

MATERIALS

1 place mat for clutch bag *or* 2 mats for shoulder bag

matching thread

cotton print fabric for lining

12″ heavy-duty zipper[18] for clutch

cord[21] for handle of shoulder bag (dyed to match if necessary)

METHOD I — The Clutch

Step 1

With place mat in a vertical position, right side down, measure and mark in one-third divisions with pins. Bring up lower edge of the mat, folding on the one-third line. Sew sides together either by hand or machine. (See fig. 1.)

Step 2

Make the zippered lining. Cut two pieces of material to conform to the inside of the bag plus ⅝″ seam allowance on all sides. Apply the zipper at top edges so that it faces out from the wrong side of the material. With right sides together, sew side and bottom seams. Press. With thread and needle tack lining to inside of bag.

METHOD II — The Shoulder Bag

Step 1

With the place mats in a vertical position, fold over the top two corners of both mats. Press with warm iron and stitch ½″ away from fold edge. Trim to ¾″ from fold edge.

Step 3

With wrong sides together, topstitch around sides and bottom of mats, ending where triangles are folded over.

Step 3

If you want to line the bag, follow the instructions in Method I up to the zipper application. Fold top edges down ⅝″ onto wrong side of fabric and press. Set aside.

Step 4

Make the handles. Form eight 24″ lengths of cord and cover the lengths with a series of simple loops. (See fig. 2.) After you have covered the cord, knot ends securely. Repeat the process for the other handle. Fasten the handles securely to the inside of the bag with a series of hand stitches.

Step 5

Slipstitch the lining in place. If you choose not to line the bag, cover the ends of the handles by gluing a piece of leather or stitching a patch of fabric over them.

VARIATIONS

The endless variety of place mats available permits you to make an endless variety of bags—quilted, calico, canvas, plastic.

Use the place mats horizontally and attach longer handles for another great look.

Use canvas strips instead of cord for the handles or braid lengths of cord to form handles.

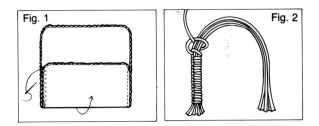

Fig. 1

Fig. 2

FAT COOKIES

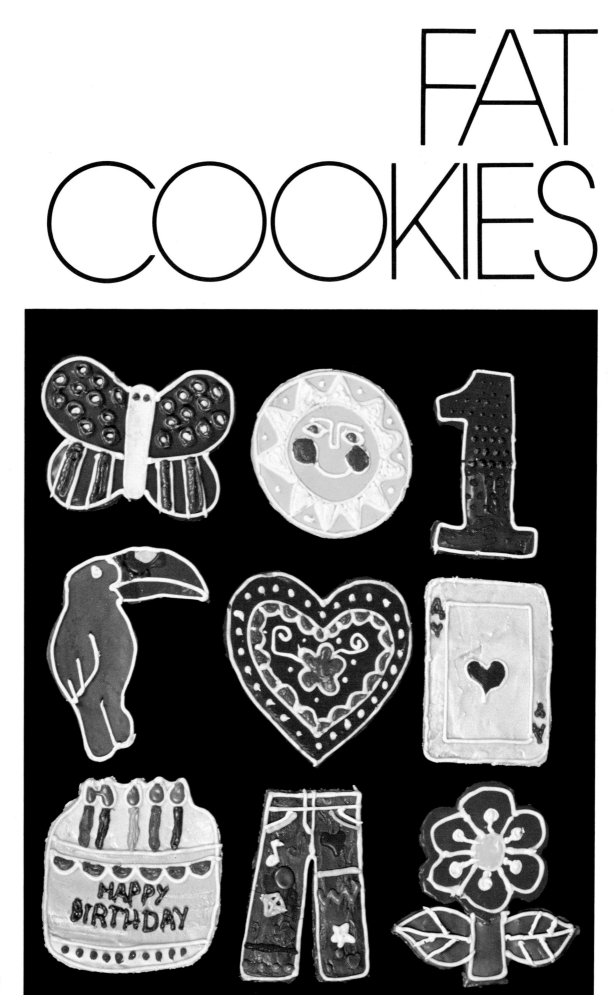

Delightful to look at, delicious to eat, Fat Cookies seem to please everyone, young or old. Wrap them in bright paper, tie them with ribbons, make special cookies for special occasions, special people. Just follow the simple method below and wait for the smiles.

MATERIALS

wax paper

recipe cookie dough

sifter

rolling pin

pencil

carbon paper

cardboard for cookie pattern

scissors

flour

sharp knife

baking sheet

cake rack or paper towels

blender or mixer

three eggs

cream of tartar

1 lb. confectioners' sugar

a few small bowls

food-coloring paste[7]

metal spatula

pastry tube with outline tip[7]

RECIPE

SUGAR COOKIES

2 ½ cups flour

½ teaspoon salt

2 teaspoons baking powder

¾ cup sugar

2 eggs, beaten

1 teaspoon vanilla

1 tablespoon milk

Sift flour, salt, baking powder; cream shortening and sugar and add eggs and vanilla. Add flour mixture and milk. Chill. Bake on ungreased cookie sheet at 375° 10–15 minutes.

Yield : 5 to 7 cookies

METHOD

Step 1

Between two pieces of wax paper, roll to ½″ thickness the dough from the recipe above or from your favorite sugar or gingerbread cookie recipe.

Step 2

Using tracing paper, trace cookie patterns on page 156 and with carbon paper transfer to cardboard, cut out and dust lightly with flour.

Step 3

Remove top sheet of wax paper from dough and place pattern on top. Cut around edges with a sharp knife.

Step 4

After all the cookies have been cut, remove excess dough and cut the wax paper between them with scissors. Slip your hand under the wax paper, flip the cookies onto a baking sheet and remove the wax paper. Reroll the excess dough for extra cookies.

Step 5

Bake the cookies until firm and cool on a rack or on paper towels.

Step 6

Now make the icing. The following recipe turns fairly hard and is especially good for decorating cookies. Use a blender or mixer to beat 3 egg whites and ½ teaspoon cream of tartar until frothy. Sift 1 pound confectioners' sugar into a bowl and slowly add egg mixture. If the resulting mixture is too thick, thin with a beaten egg white and a pinch of cream of tartar or with water.

Step 7

Divide the icing into bowls, one for each color you will use, and save some white for outlining. Carefully tint each portion the shade you desire. The best colors come from food-coloring paste. Regular liquid food coloring will produce a nice yellow, a decent pink, a terrible purple and an unpleasant green.

Step 8

Make sure the icing is thin enough to coat the cookies smoothly. With a spatula, quickly ice the cookies with the main color or colors. (Remember, if you apply the icing too slowly, it will start to dry as you ice and will form lumps.)

Step 9

Use a simple outline tip and pastry tube to trace all outlines and details in white (or red if you prefer). Fill in all other colors and let dry. You will have Fat Cookies that sparkle with fun!

VARIATIONS

Fat Cookies make charming Christmas-tree decorations. Punch a hole in each cookie, bake, decorate and shellac for durability. Thread a ribbon or tinsel cord through the hole and hang your decoration on the tree.

Try other patterns for special occasions—a mortar board for a graduation or a Teddy bear or rattle for a baby shower.

BRAIDED BASKETS

The baskets pictured here are formed from braids of raffia that are sewn together. Raffia baskets make inexpensive decorative containers with a variety of uses. Arrange dried flowers or fruit in a medium-sized basket, use a large one as a planter, smaller ones to hold cigarettes, matches or candy on your coffee table.

MATERIALS

1 lb. raffia[5] in assorted colors
one spool carpet thread each in coordinating colors
needle
bowl or box for shaping basket (optional)
scissors
upholstery needle (optional)

METHOD

Step 1

Divide the raffia into groups with five to six strands of the same color to a group.

Step 2

Firmly braid together two groups of the same color with one group of another color. Make eight to ten of these braids for a medium-sized basket. (For example, braid two groups of green with one of orange.)

Step 3

Firmly braid together three groups of another color combination. Make several of these braids.

Step 4

Using the photograph as a guide for color choice, make the base of the basket. First decide on the shape basket you wish to make. Then form a coil in the proper shape by stitching the braid together with needle and carpet thread. (See fig. 1.) Switch color combinations, using photograph as a guide. Continue coiling the braid until you have made a base of the desired size. (To join ends of the braids, fold ends on a diagonal and overcast stitch the two together as shown in fig. 2.)

Step 5

Make the sides of the basket by sewing the bottom edge of one coil to the top edge of the preceding coil. (See fig. 3.) Keep building the coil and stitching it together until you have reached the desired height. (You might find it helpful to form the basket around a bowl or a box.) Finish by trimming ends of raffia, folding them in at an angle and securing with several stitches. (See fig. 4.) Sew sides to base using an overcast stitch. You might find using a curved upholstery needle easier than a straight one.

Step 6

Make a handle by sewing two or three braids together and attaching the ends of the braid to the inner sides of the basket. Finish off the handles by folding up the ends, wrapping with a strand of raffia and knotting or securing with a few stitches. (See fig. 5.)

Step 7

Make a lid, if you wish, by following the instructions for the base of the basket (step 4) but making the lid slightly larger than the base. Add a few rows of braid coming down from the top to form sides. (See fig. 6.)

VARIATIONS

Make raffia coasters, place mats or area rugs.
Make place mats and use the instructions on page 14 to make Place-Mat Purses.

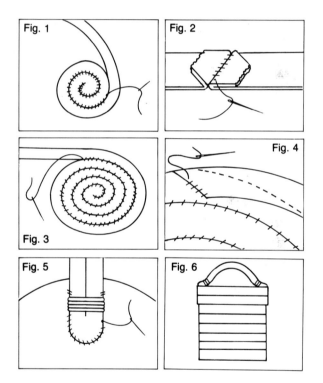

Fig. 1

Fig. 2

Fig. 3

Fig. 4

Fig. 5

Fig. 6

BATH
ROBE

This terrycloth robe will be a bright spot in your morning. The neon colors are cheering even on the bleakest day. The robe pictured here was made for Dick several years ago and has weathered wear and tear beautifully. I made another one for Dad, and Jay is still waiting for his. Buy a lot of fabric, for you'll probably use it filling the robe orders of all your friends. If you prefer, you may use towels for your material.

MATERIALS

pencil

tracing paper

terrycloth: 1⅝ yds. yellow, 2 yds. bright green, 1 yd. hot pink, ½ yd. cobalt blue[10]

scissors

dressmaker's carbon

pins

thread

sewing machine

yardstick

METHOD

Step 1

Follow the instructions on page 150 to enlarge the pattern on page 160 and, with dressmaker's carbon, transfer to paper and cut out. Because this is a wrap robe and not meant to fit sleekly, one size should fit all but the tiniest or largest person. Alter size at side seams, adding or subtracting width there. Remember that sizes vary by ½" on all seams. Adjust pattern sleeve and robe length before cutting.

Step 2

Pin enlarged pattern pieces to terrycloth—back and two front pieces on the green cloth; one sleeve on the blue; the other sleeve and the pocket on the pink; the star, tie belt, belt carriers and contrasting band on the yellow. Cut out.

Step 3

Zigzag all edges to prevent fraying or sew flat fell seams.

Step 4

Press under pocket edges ⅝" and topstitch ½" from edge. Pin star to center of pocket and baste securely. Zigzag a satin stitch around edges. (See fig. 1.) Pin pocket along pocket line on left front. Stitch ½" from edge, reinforcing stitching at upper corners. (See fig. 2.)

Step 5

Stitch the front and back at shoulders.

Step 6

Stitch back seam of band sections. Press under raw edges ½". Place right side of band on wrong side of robe. Pin and stitch front and neck edges. Trim seam and press toward band. Turn band to outside and press. Stitch folded edge over seam. (See fig. 3.)

Step 7

With right sides together, pin sleeve to armhole edge, baste, stitch and press seam open.

Step 8

With right sides together, pin front to back at side seams and pin sleeve seams. Stitch side and sleeve seams. Press up sleeve hems 2" and slipstitch. Topstitch ½" from sleeve edge.

Step 9

Try on and mark length. Make a shirt-tail hem by folding raw edge of hem under ¼" and pressing. Then fold under ½" and topstitch.

Step 10

Make the tie belt. Fold belt in half lengthwise, right sides together. Stitch ends and length with a ½" seam allowance, leaving a 4" opening. Trim seams and turn belt right side out. Slipstitch opening.

Step 11

Make the belt carriers. Press under edges of belt carriers ¼", fold in half lengthwise and topstitch. Sew carriers to side seam, edges in.

VARIATIONS

Make a classic robe in a solid color.

Try a long version and vary the colors.

Sew a motif on the back and make a wrestler's robe.

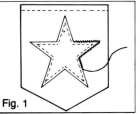

Fig. 1

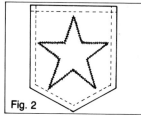

Fig. 2

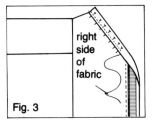

Fig. 3

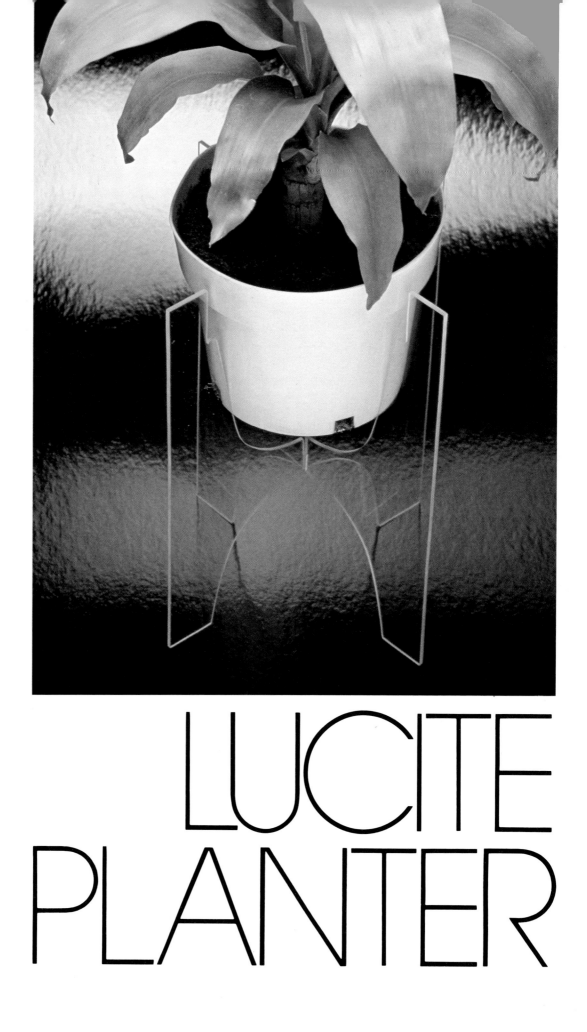

LUCITE PLANTER

Put your favorite plants in a lucite plant stand. The clear, stark lucite provides a complementary contrast to leafy greenery and decorative pots. Lucite is not difficult to work with, and it is exciting to use.

MATERIALS

pencil

10″ × 25″ large piece of paper

scissors

adhesive paper (optional)

two 10″ × 12″ pieces of 7/16″ clear lucite[11]

1 sheet each coarse, medium, fine and very fine sandpaper

jigsaw or saber saw with metal blades[16]

1 bottle acrylic glue[11],[16] (optional)

METHOD

Step 1

Using the instructions on page 150, enlarge pattern on this page on paper. Cut out pattern carefully with scissors. (The pattern given here is for a 10″ × 12″ stand. If you wish to make a stand that is larger or smaller, alter the pattern accordingly.)

Step 2

Most lucite comes with a protective paper covering; leave it on the lucite until the stand is completed. The paper protects the surface from damage while you are working and helps to keep the edges from chipping during sawing. If your plastic comes without paper on it, cover it with adhesive paper. With pencil, transfer pattern lines to the paper covering. Very carefully and slowly, cut out pattern shapes and notches from lucite with a saw.

Step 3

Carefully sand edges with the sandpaper, starting with the coarsest to the finest.

Step 4

Assemble plant stand, placing one piece over the other, fitting notches. Glue if you wish, following bottle directions. The stand will stay together without glue, but glue makes it a bit more sturdy. Let dry and you are ready to place your potted plants in the stand.

VARIATIONS

Use leftover pieces of plastic to make napkin rings. Cut plastic in strips, hold strips in hot water until they bend and then shape them around a broom handle.

Make a lucite bracelet. Laminate two pieces of clear lucite with a translucent color in between (using acrylic glue) and cut out a bracelet following the instructions for Wooden Bracelets on page 124.

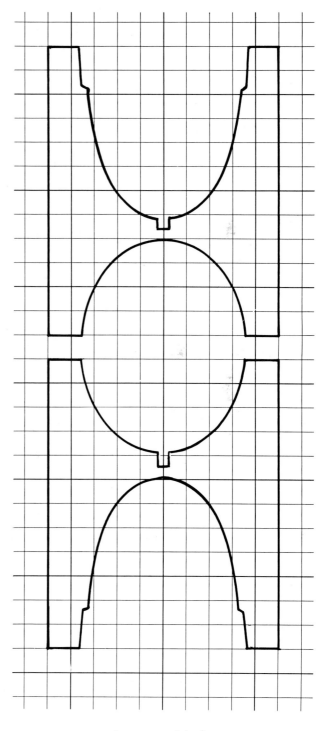

1 square = 1 inch

WORK
SWEATER

Here is a sweater version of the classic work shirt.
Knitted of denim-look worsted, it is trimmed with
multicolored blanket stitching. Knit it in a wardrobe
of colors or make the dress version with the instructions I have included.

MATERIALS

six 4-oz. skeins of denim-look blue knitting worsted[1],[17] (Method I)

ten 4-oz. skeins of denim-look blue knitting worsted[1],[17] (Method II)

1 pair #6 (Canadian #8) knitting needles or any size needles that will give a gauge of 5 stitches = 1″ in stockinette stitch

blue thread

sewing machine or needle with large eye

twelve ½″ red buttons (Method I)

sixteen ½″ red buttons (Method II)

1 skein of needlepoint, tapestry or crewel yarn in each of the following colors: yellow, turquoise, pink, green, magenta, red

METHOD I—The Shirt-Sweater

Step 1

The purl side of the stockinette stitch is the right side of the sweater. The directions given here are for a size 10 sweater. Changes for sizes 12, 14 and 16 are in parentheses. Make the back. (See knitting instructions, stitches and abbreviations on page 151.) Cast on 80 (86, 92, 98) sts and k every row for 5 rows.

Row 6: p across.

Row 7: k across.

Repeat rows 6 and 7 until piece measures 9″ from cast-on edge. Inc 1 st at beg and end of next row. Repeat incs after 3 more inches. Work even until the piece measures 15″ or desired length to underarm.

Step 2

Shape the arm holes. Bind off 6 (7, 7, 7) sts at beg of next 2 rows. Then k 2 sts tog at beg and end of every other row 6 (6, 6, 7) times—60 (64, 70, 74) sts. Work even until armholes measure 7¼ (7½, 7¾, 8) inches from first bind-off straight up to needle.

Step 3

Shape the shoulders. At the beg of next 4 rows, bind off 7 (7, 7, 8) sts. At the beg of the next row bind off 5 (6, 8, 8) sts. Bind off remaining 22 (24, 26, 26) sts.

Step 4

Make the right front. Cast on 44 (48, 50, 54) sts. Knit every row for 5 rows.

Row 6: k 8 (front band), put a marker on needle, k 36 (40, 42, 46).

Row 7: p to marker, slip marker, k 8.

Row 8: k 8, slip marker, k to end of row.

Repeat rows 7 and 8, increasing 1 st at side edge after 9″ and once again after 3″. Work even on 46 (50, 52, 56) sts until piece is the same length as back from bottom edge to underarm. End on wrong side row.

Step 5

Shape the armhole. Bind off 6 (7, 7, 7) sts at beg of next row at armhole edge. Then k 2 tog at beg of next 6 (6, 6, 7) rows at armhole edge. Work even on 34 (37, 39, 42) sts until armhole measures 4¼ (4½, 4¾, 5) inches, ending with a right side row.

Step 6

Shape the neck. At front edge, bind off 12 (14, 14, 15) sts (removing marker), k to end of row. Dec 1 st at same edge every other row 3 times. Work even on 19 (20, 22, 24) sts until armhole measures 7¼ (7½, 7¾, 8) inches.

Step 7

Shape the shoulders. At beg of next 2 rows at armhole edge, bind off 7 (7, 7, 8) sts. At beg of next row at armhole edge, bind off remaining 5 (6, 8, 8) sts.

Step 8

Make the left front. Work to correspond to right front, reversing all shaping and placement of front band and forming first buttonhole when piece measures 1½″. Buttonhole: starting at front edge, k 3, bind off next 2 sts. Work to end of row, on the next row, cast on 2 sts over those bound off in previous row. Make 5 more buttonholes evenly spaced, the last one being 1″ from bound-off sts.

Step 9

Make the sleeves. (Make 2.) Cast on 40 (44, 50, 54) and work in stockinette st for 1″. Inc 1 st at beg and end of next row. Repeat inc row every inch 8 (8, 9, 9) times. Work even on 56 (60, 66, 70) sts until piece measures 15½″ or desired length to underarm. Shape cap: at beg of next 2 rows bind off 6 (7, 7, 7) sts, k 2 tog at beg and end of every other row until 18 sts remain. Then bind off 2 sts at the beg of every row until 10 sts are left; bind off remaining sts.

Step 10

Make the cuffs. (Make 2.) Cast on 46 (50, 56, 58) sts. Work in garter st (k every row) for 2½″, working 2 buttonholes (evenly spaced) on one end of each cuff. Bind off.

Step 11

Make the collar. Cast on 72 sts, working in garter st, inc 1 st each end of needle every other row 15 times. Bind off.

Step 12

Make the pockets. Cast on 26 sts, work in stockinette st for 5½″, purling first and last st on all k rows and knitting first and last st on all p rows. End with a k row. Flap: k next row. Continue in garter st for 1". Dec 1 st at each end every row until 3 sts remain. Bind off.

Step 13

Finish the sweater. Sew shoulder, underarm and sleeve seams. Set in sleeves. These seams can be sewn on a sewing machine or by hand with a backstitch, right sides together. Sew the collar to neck edge, starting and ending it ½" from front edges. Sew cuffs to sleeves. The seams for the cuffs and the collar can be sewn with an overcast st by hand. Sew pockets in place (see picture). Finish buttonholes with a single crochet or buttonhole stitch around each hole. Sew on buttons. Outline collar, cuffs, armholes, shoulders and placket with a blanket stitch (see embroidery glossary on page 000), using the photograph as a color and placement guide. Block, using the measurements below. Size 10 (12, 14, 16): bust = 34" (36", 38", 40").

METHOD II—The Sweater-Dress

Step 1

The purl side of the stockinette stitch is the right side of the sweater. The directions given here are for a size 10 dress. Changes for sizes 12, 14 and 16 are in parentheses. Make the back. (See knitting instructions, stitches and abbreviations on page 151.) Cast on 120 (125, 130, 135) sts and k every row for 5 rows. Change to the stockinette st (k 1 row, p 1 row, k the next, etc.) and work even for 3", ending on p row. *K 22 (23, 24, 25), k next 2 sts tog, place a marker on needle*, repeat from * across row—5 decs made, 5 markers on needle. Continue to work in stockinette st, slipping markers as you work. Dec again by knitting 2 sts tog in front of each marker every 3" 4 more times—95 (100, 105, 110) sts. Work even until piece measures 15¾ (16, 16¼, 16½) inches. Make any adjustments for length now—see blocking measurements for planned skirt length. Work 1 more inch even, ending on p row. Dec by knitting 2 sts tog before each marker across row—5 decs made. Repeat this row 1 more time after 2". Size 10: repeat dec row again after 2"—80 sts. Size 12: repeat dec row again after 2" but do not dec at one of the markers—86 sts. Size 14: repeat dec row again after 2" but do not dec at 2 of the markers—92 sts. Size 16: repeat dec row again after 2" but do not dec at 3 of the markers—98 sts. Remove markers and work even until piece measures 24¾ (25, 25¼, 25½) inches. Mark for waist. Continue in stockinette st until you are 4" above waist. Inc 1 st at beg and end of next row. Repeat incs after 3" more. Work even until piece measured from waist is desired length to underarm.

Step 2

Shape the armholes following the instructions in Method I, step 2.

Step 3

Make the right front. Cast on 64 (66, 70, 72) sts and k every row for 5 rows. Next row: k 8, place marker on needle, k 56 (58, 62, 64). Next row: p to marker, k 8. These 8 stitches are your front band and must always be knitted, while the rest of the piece is worked in stockinette stitch. Work even until piece measures 2½" from beg. End on a p row. Next row: k 8, sl marker, *k 26 (27, 29, 30), k 2 tog, place marker on needle*, repeat from * across row—2 decs made, 3 markers on needle. Work even for 2½", ending on p row. Dec row: k 8, sl marker, *k to within 2 sts of next marker, k 2 tog*, repeat from * 1 more time. Repeat dec row every 2½" 4 more times—52 (54, 58, 60) sts. Work even until piece measures 15¾ (16, 16¼, 16½) inches from beg. Work even 1" more. Repeat dec row every 1½" 4 (3, 4, 3) times. Remove dec markers (not front-band marker) and work even until piece measures 24¾ (25, 25¼, 25½) inches. Mark for waist. Continue in stockinette st until you are 4" above waist—inc 1 st at side seam edge. Repeat inc after 3" more. Work even until piece is same length as back.

Step 4

Shape the armhole following the instructions in Method I, step 5. Mark the right front for button placement, having the first button 1" from neck edge and the last button 6" from bottom.

Step 5

Make the left front following the instructions for the right front but reversing all shaping and the placement of the front band. Form buttonholes to match the markers on right front following the instructions in Method I, step 8.

Step 6

Make the sleeves, cuffs, collar and pockets following the instructions in Method I, steps 9, 10, 11, 12, 13.

Step 7

Finish the dress following the instructions in Method I, step 14, but use the blocking measurements below. Size 10 (12, 14, 16): hips—38 (40, 42, 44) inches; skirt length from waist—24¾ (25, 25¼, 25½) inches.

RUG COAT

A lightweight wool rug is the basis for this one-of-a-kind coat. Rugs often have lovely, subtle patterns in rich colors that coordinate beautifully with winter clothes. Ann made the one pictured here from an inexpensive rug found in an antique store that proved to be not only attractive but warm as well. The versatile pattern for the coat can also be used to make the great wrap dress shown here in denim. Making the coat or dress is a breeze, because one size fits (almost) all, and there are no zippers or buttons.

MATERIALS

tracing paper

pencil

dressmaker's carbon

stiff paper for pattern

scissors

a lightweight woven wool rug at least 5′ x 7′ or 2½ yds. of fabric 45″ wide or 3 yds. of fabric 36″ wide

matching thread

sewing machine

pins

3 yds. matching 1″ bias tape for facing

METHOD

Step 1

Using tracing paper, trace the pattern on page 161 and with carbon transfer to stiff paper. Following the instructions on page 150, enlarge the pattern. Because this is a wrap coat and not meant to fit snugly, one size should fit all. If you are very small or very large, alter size at side seams, adding or subtracting a size in ½″ steps. Adjust the sleeve length and hem length on the pattern before cutting.

Step 2

Cut two of each pattern piece from stiff paper. (Each piece will be cut individually on a single thickness of the rug.) Place pattern pieces on the right side of the rug, making the most of the pattern design. Try several arrangements and select the best. Pin pattern pieces down and cut out carefully. It will save time if you use your sewing machine's throat-plate measurements as a guide for your ⅝″ seam allowance rather than marking it on each piece. If your machine doesn't have measurements on the throat-plate, place a piece of tape ⅝″ from the needle and use as a guide. Be sure all seam allowances are the same.

Step 3

With right sides together and matching notches, sew side seams and shoulder seams. (See fig. 1.) Press with iron set for wool. Sew sleeve seams and press flat. Press edge of sleeve under ⅝″. Fold sleeve edge under the amount shown on pattern and machine topstitch on right side. Fold sleeve edge up to form cuff. (See fig. 2.) Do other sleeve.

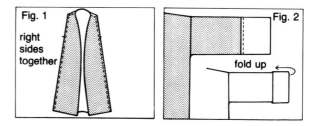

Fig. 1
right sides together

Fig. 2
fold up

Step 4

Fit sleeve into armhole, pin or baste and stitch. Press.

Step 5

With right sides together, pin bias tape to front and neck edges of the coat. Machine stitch and press seam toward coat. Turn tape to the inside and tack so that the tape doesn't show on the outside of the coat. (See fig. 3.)

Step 6

Make the tie belt. Stitch pieces together, fold in half lengthwise (right sides together) and stitch all around, leaving a 4″ opening. Press, turn belt right side out, slipstitch opening and press.

Step 7

Try on coat with belt tied and mark hemline. Trim to within 2½″ of hemline. Overcast raw edge either by hand or with a machine zigzag stitch. With the machine's top tension fairly loose, stay stitch around the coat bottom, ¼″ to ½″ from the edge. Pull ends of thread, shirring slightly to ease out unwanted fullness. Slide a piece of paper between hem edge and coat and press with steam iron. (See fig. 4.) (The paper prevents the edge from marking the outside of the coat.) Stitch a row of basting ¾″ from hem edge through both thicknesses and fold back for hemming. (See fig. 5.) Sew the hem in place with tiny, well-spaced stitches. Make sure stitching does not show on the right side. Remove basting and you have an invisible hem.

Step 8

Topstitch cuff, front and hem edges if you wish. The dress as shown has a row of straight stitching and a row of zigzag in rust-colored thread.

VARIATIONS

Line the coat with sunback satin for extra warmth.

Make a coat out of a patchwork quilt or blanket.

Make a bathrobe by cutting the pattern from terrycloth and making it ankle-length.

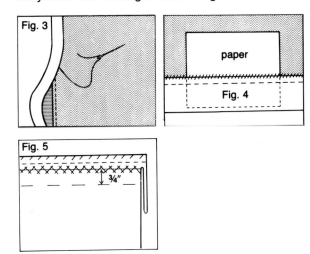

Fig. 3

paper
Fig. 4

Fig. 5

¾″

ANTIQUE PHOTOS

Lend an air of nostalgia to your favorite black-and-white snapshots by making them look like old-fashioned daguerreotypes. The method is simple, quick and inexpensive and the results are a pleasant change from color.

MATERIALS

2 shallow glass or plastic containers or dishes

regular-strength coffee or tea or sepia toner from a photographic supply house

black-and-white photograph (the darker the exposure the better). Use special care with one-of-a-kind photos. The paper occasionally curls, damaging the photo.

white paper towels

2 cookie sheets

several heavy books or bricks

tracing paper

soft pencil

mat knife.

8″ × 10″ piece of heavy manila paper[2]

sepia ink[2]

lettering pen with fine tip[2]

oval frame to fit photograph or antique frame

METHOD

Step 1

Fill one container with about 1″ of warm water (75°–80°) and the other with about 1″ of tea or coffee. (If you use sepia toner, follow the package directions for the entire process.)

Step 2

Presoak photograph in water tray for about 15 minutes or longer. Then soak in coffee or tea for about 1 minute. Rinse in water tray. If the photo is not dark enough, repeat process.

Step 3

Blot photo thoroughly with paper towels. Line a cookie sheet with two thicknesses of paper towels. Put picture on sheet. Place another sheet on top and put heavy books or bricks on the photo to weigh it down. (This is to insure that the paper dries flat, for photographs have a tendency to curl.)

Step 4

With tracing paper, trace an oval with decorative lines on this page that will fit over your photo. With a soft lead pencil retrace lines. Turn right side of paper over on manila paper and pencil over lines to transfer them. Carefully using a lettering pen and tip, ink in lines. I suggest practicing first. Never load pen too full. Always make a stroke on scrap paper before inking the manila. Cut out oval with mat knife. Tape oval over photograph on wrong side and slip into frame. Or, take a short cut by mounting photo under an undecorated mat and inserting in an antique frame.

VARIATIONS

Dress in period costume and strike a stiff, old-fashioned pose for the basis of a really authentic-looking daguerreotype.

Use the photos as parts of old-fashioned valentines. Cut mats of brown construction paper and edge with white lace.

enlarge if necessary

MOM'S BEANS

As far as I'm concerned, the following recipe makes what may be the world's best beans. Put them on the stove while you're making another project and earn a reputation for being able to do two things at once successfully!

MATERIALS

1 lb. pinto beans
colander
6-qt. waterless pot with lid
2 qts. cold water
¼ lb. salt pork (cured)
salt
¼ to ½ cup chili powder
3 cloves garlic, mashed
1 medium onion, freshly chopped
pinch of sugar

METHOD

Step 1
Carefully sort through pinto beans for small stones. Rinse beans thoroughly in a colander.

Step 2
Pour beans into a six-quart pot with two quarts of cold water. Add sliced salt pork and cover. Bring to a boil, then reduce heat and simmer for about one and a half hours or until tender. Add more water if needed. (It is very important that the water be cold to begin with and that the beans be simmered. These factors make it possible to use the beans without soaking them overnight.)

Step 3
After the beans have simmered, turn up the heat and quickly bring to a boil again. This will cause some of the beans to burst, forming a thick juice. If the juice is too thick, add more water; if too thin, simmer longer.

Step 4
Stir beans occasionally to prevent them from sticking. Add chili powder, garlic, onion and sugar. Cook rapidly five to ten minutes more. Add salt to taste. You now have something worth breaking your diet for.

Mom's Beans are great for picnics and barbecues. My mother serves them with hot cornbread or rice, sliced tomatoes and green onions.

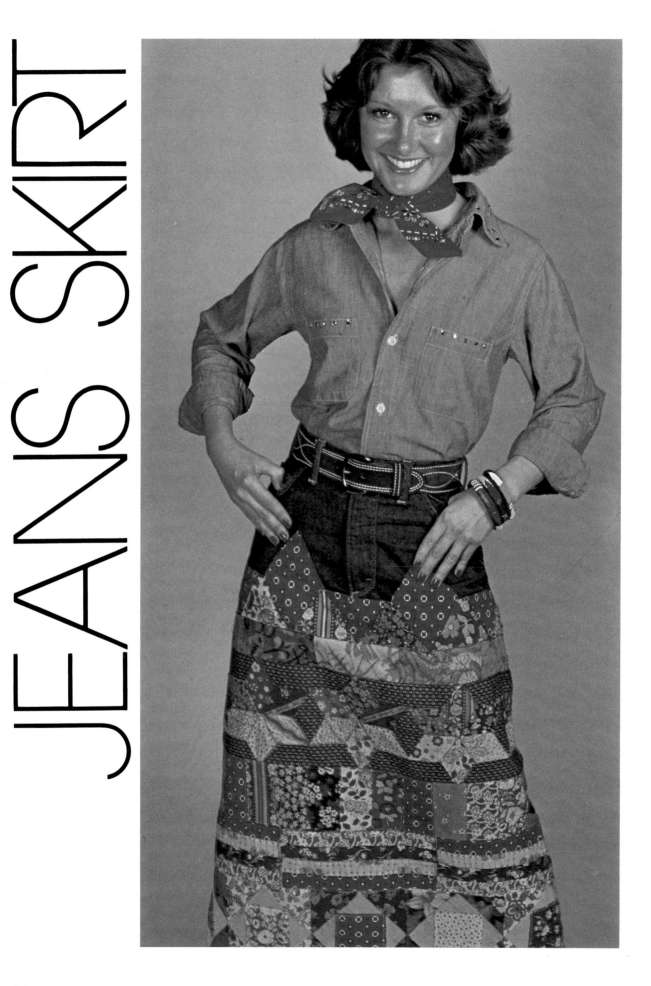

JEANS SKIRT

This Jeans Skirt has great versatility; it can be dressed up or down. It looks as well with a sweater and tights or funny socks as it does with a skinny T-shirt and sandals. I sketched the skirt for my friend Kathy to make, and she did such a great job that she is frequently asked by envious admirers if she will sell it.

MATERIALS

1 pair of worn-out jeans

tracing paper

paper for pattern

pencil

carbon paper

calico and gingham pieces (sewing leftovers, remnants or about ten ¼ yd. lengths of various calico and gingham prints), colorfast and pre-shrunk[10]

scissors

iron

1½ yds. colorful sturdy calico for background, 45″ wide or wider, colorfast, preshrunk[10]

pins

yardstick

tailor's chalk

1 to 2 spools of red thread

sewing machine

1 skein red cotton embroidery thread[1] (optional)

METHOD

Step 1

Measure 1″ (seam allowance) below jeans' fly and cut straight across. (See fig. 1.) Cut long 4″ wide strips from the legs and set aside. Most jeans are fitted at the hip; if you want your skirt fitted at the waist, alter now.

Step 2

Using tracing paper, trace the patterns on page 162 and with carbon transfer to paper and use to cut out patchwork pieces. Press edges of patches under ¼″ and set aside.

Step 3

Cut background calico in half (two 27″ lengths) and mark a 1″ seam allowance on top of each piece. Pin calico to jeans just below fly.

Step 4

With pencil or chalk and yardstick make a line from side seam of jeans to ½″ from selvage edge at bottom of fabric. (This forms the "A" of your skirt.)

Add ½″ seam allowance (see fig. 2) and trim excess. Unpin calico from jeans. Using the front as a pattern, cut the remaining piece of calico for back.

Step 5

Using the photograph as a guide, pin the patchwork pieces on right side of calico, occasionally letting the calico show through. Some pieces will extend beyond the seam and should be trimmed later.

Step 6

Sew down pieces, using straight machine or hand embroidery stitch.

Step 7

When both front and back are finished put right sides together and baste along the seam lines. Then baste skirt to jeans top. Try on and correct fit. Remove basting stitches that hold top and skirt together, machine-stitch side seams, stitch skirt to jeans, trim all seams and press.

Step 8

To form the hem, stitch the 4″-wide strips of denim together until they measure the circumference of the skirt plus 1″ (½″ seam allowance on each end). Sew right sides of ends together on ½″ seam allowance. Press in half. Slip raw edges under last row of patchwork and topstitch. Your skirt is finished. To keep it in good shape, dry clean it or wash by hand in cold water.

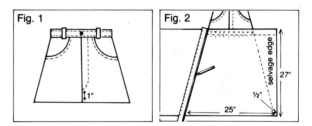

MELON CLUTCH

Make this handbag for your whimsical moods. The colorful Watermelon Clutch is made from suede and is sewn by machine with a leather needle.

MATERIALS

pencil

tracing paper

carbon paper

stiff paper or cardboard

suede[5]:12″ × 13″ red, 14″ square yellow, 16″ × 11″ green and 3″ square black

scissors

¼ yd. of 36″ lightweight black cotton fabric for backing

contact cement

black thread

16″ industrial zipper in red

sewing machine with needle for sewing leather

METHOD

Step 1

Using the method on page 150, enlarge the pattern on this page and trace to stiff paper or cardboard.

Step 2

Cut two of each pattern piece: "A" in red suede, "B" in yellow and "C" in green. Place pattern pieces on the suede, trace around the edges with a pencil and cut along pencil line. Mark seed placement on the two "A" pieces and cut out seeds from black suede.

Step 3

Fit and glue suede pieces to the backing, making sure that no edges overlap. (See fig. 1.) Glue seeds to the red suede. Let dry. Trim backing around the watermelon so that it is flush with the suede.

Step 4

Zigzag all the edges of the watermelon sections in black thread. (See fig. 2.) Straight stitch around the edges of the seeds.

Step 5

Apply the zipper to the top edges of the watermelon.

Step 6

Stitch around watermelon edge to finish. If your sewing machine will not sew leather, have your shoe repairman stitch the clutch or make holes with an awl and stitch with a leather needle and heavy black thread.

VARIATIONS

The Watermelon Clutch can be made in heavy cotton instead of suede. Follow the instructions above but allow a ½″ seam allowance around all pieces. Sew all the seams to the inside and make a separate lining.

Make a "slice" of orange or lemon clutch or make a shoulder bag.

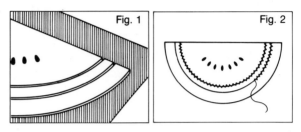

enlarge twice (see page 150)

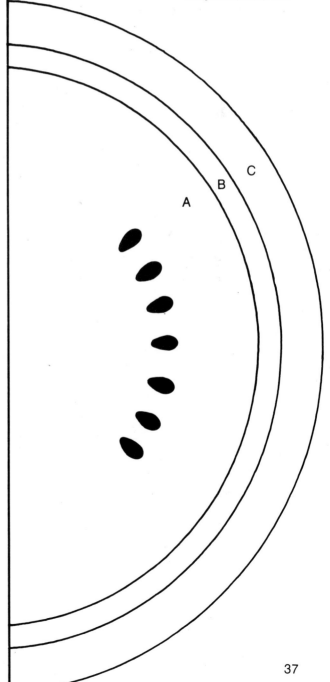

MACRAME SHAWL

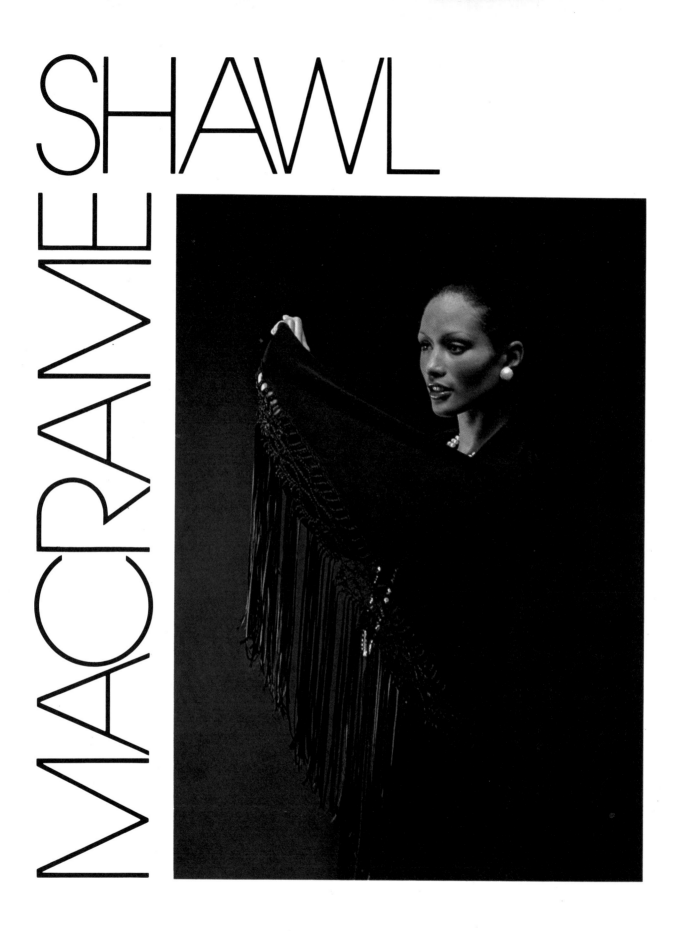

Make this luxuriously fringed Macramé Shawl for evening. Lois showed me that macramé is surprisingly uncomplicated, and this project is an exciting way to learn the craft.

MATERIALS

1 hemmed 56" × 40" × 40" triangle of black matte (or nylon) jersey

3 large spools of ¼" black rayon ribbon[1]

1 spool of black thread

pins

needle

scissors

ruler

METHOD

Step 1

Cut ribbon into strips 72" long, fold strips in half and sew on fold to the 40" edges of the shawl at approximately ¾" intervals, making sure that the final number of strips sewn is divisible by eight. (Marking the shawl edges for ribbon placement with pins first lets you adjust the spacing, if necessary.)

Step 2

See accompanying diagrams for knots and stitches. Tie each piece of ribbon with a slip knot. From this point on, work from the left-hand side of shawl. Use "working thread" to make three spiral-staircase stitches.

Step 3

Make three half hitches on working thread and repeat steps 2 and 3 across edge of shawl.

Step 4

The thread that is now on the left-hand side becomes the working thread. Make three more half hitches on this thread. Work across shawl.

Step 5

Join the right-hand thread of the first group to the left-hand thread of the next with a half hitch that is in line with the three half hitches just made.

Step 6

Working with four groups, or 16 threads, drape working thread so that it forms a scallop 2" at widest part measured from the last row of half hitches. Connect working thread to 16th thread with a half hitch right under row of half hitches. Make half hitches on working thread with the threads it crosses. Work across the shawl in the same manner.

Step 7

Lay shawl flat and bring leftmost thread in line with edge of shawl. Drape the 8th thread in a half scallop and tie with half hitch to leftmost thread. Tie half hitches on this thread with the threads it crosses. (The spacing between knots will be

wider here than in other places.) Repeat same procedure in reverse for the right-hand side.

Step 8

Take the 9th thread in the first group, drape to form a scallop as above and tie with a half hitch to the 9th thread in the next group. Make half hitches on this thread with the threads the scallop crosses. Work across shawl.

Step 9

Repeat step 6, making sure that right and left sides of fringe stay in a line with the edges of the shawl.

Step 10

Repeat step 6 again, but leave no space between rows of knots. (See illustration for Step 1.)

Step 11

Finish shawl by tying every two strands together with a slip knot.

VARIATIONS

Sew large silk scarves into triangles and add a macramé fringe.

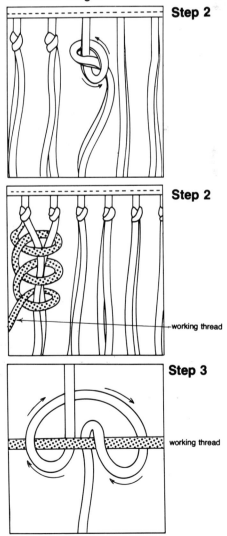

Step 2

Step 2

←working thread

Step 3

working thread

Step 3

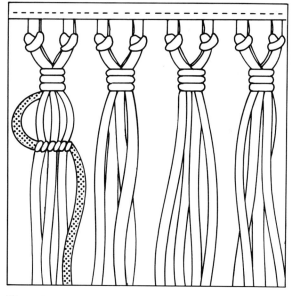

Step 4

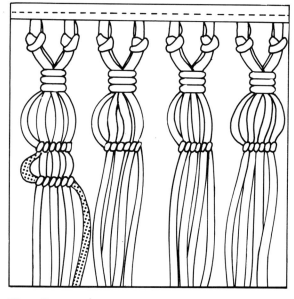

Step 5

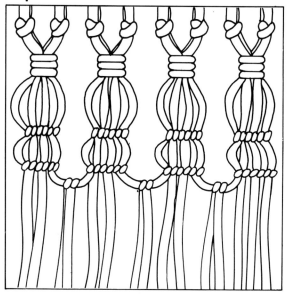

Step 6

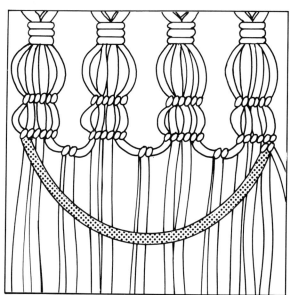

Step 7

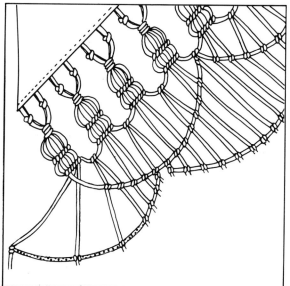

Step 8

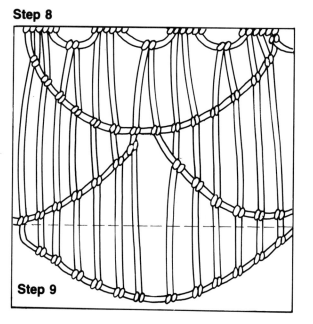

Step 9

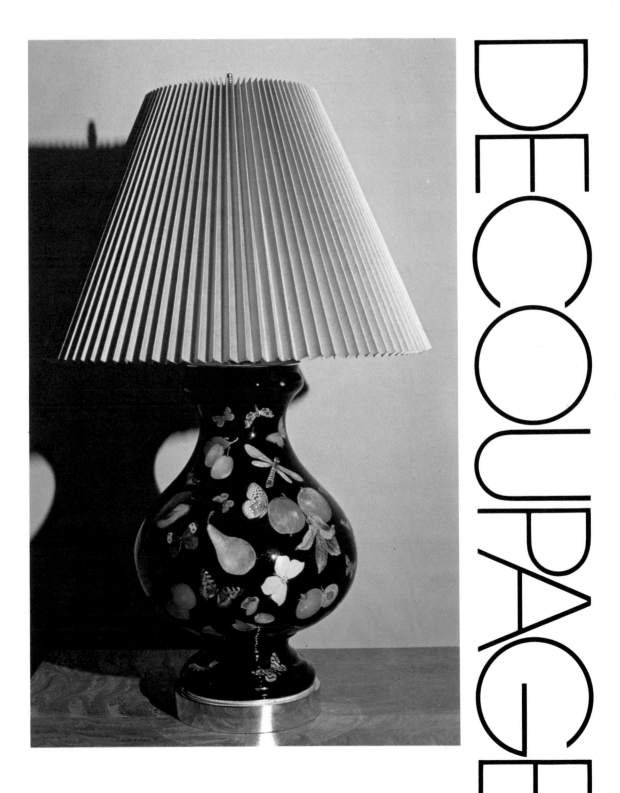

DECOUPAGE

The beautiful lamp shown here was found by my friend Gary Jones in a Manhattan shop. I asked Leta Richmond—an artist well known for her fine decoupage—for *her* method so that you can decorate objects like the lamp. The method she gave me is one that will give you professional results. It is quite simple, but it takes about three weeks from start to finish. Use magazines, old greeting cards, books, wallpaper and stationery as decoupage print sources.

MATERIALS

lamp base of just about any material

prints (as many as you wish to use for the decoupage)

clear acrylic spray[16] (optional)

dishwashing liquid (optional)

several sheets each of very fine, fine and medium sandpaper

aluminum spray[2,16] (optional)

manicure scissors

paper towels

1 pt. oil-base paint in any color you think will be an effective background for the prints you select (optional)

1 pt. new wood sealer (optional)

small container decoupage glue[2] or white glue

rolling pin or wooden roller[2]

1″ paintbrush

1 pt. flat finish varnish

1 pt. clear gloss varnish

wax paper or foil

soft, lintfree cloth

1 small container linseed oil[16]

a few tablespoons ground pumice[2]

2″ square of felt

paste wax

METHOD
Step 1

Select your prints. Try to find prints that are on very thin paper with no printing on the reverse side. If you find something you'd love to use but it is too thick, follow Leta's preparation method below:

(a) Spray front side with light coat of acrylic spray, holding the can 8″ to 10″ away from print. Let dry.

(b) Apply soap suds (from any dishwashing liquid) to the back of the print to moisten paper and sand lightly in one direction with fine sandpaper, lifting excess paper pulp as you sand. Keep the paper moist with suds only and take care that you do not rub a hole in the print. Continue until the print is sanded evenly and let dry.

If you wish to use something that has printing on the reverse side, spray the wrong side with aluminum spray.

Step 2

Carefully cut out all prints with sharp manicure scissors.

Step 3

Prepare the lamp for the decoupage. Sand the surface lightly with fine sandpaper and remove all dust with paper towels. If the lamp isn't the color you'd like, paint it with new wood sealer and follow with two coats of oil-base paint (allow 24 hours' drying time after each coat).

Step 4

Apply one print at a time to your lamp. With fingertips, spread decoupage glue generously on the back of the print. Position the print on the decoupage object and smooth the print from the center outward to remove any excess glue and to work out air bubbles. If any bubbles remain after smoothing, pierce print with a pin and push out air gently with your fingertips. Remove excess glue by gently wiping print and surrounding areas with a wet paper towel.

Step 5

Flatten the print. Cover print with a wet paper towel and roll with a rolling pin or wooden roller. Make sure that all edges are firmly glued. Apply all the prints and let dry thoroughly.

Step 6

Apply 20 coats of varnish, using flat finish varnish for the first coat, clear gloss varnish for the next 14 coats and flat finish varnish for the last five. After applying each coat place the lamp on wax paper or foil and let dry 24 hours. Dip the 1″ paintbrush into the varnish halfway and let the excess varnish drip off (do not pull off the excess on the rim of the can). Lightly brush on the varnish, in one direction, over the entire surface, lifting the brush at the end of each stroke. The tenth coat of varnish is very important. Before applying it cover the entire decoupage surface with soap suds. Sand the area lightly with a piece of medium sandpaper. Go over the entire surface several times with the sandpaper, rinse surface with water and dry thoroughly with paper towels. Wipe with a clean cloth and continue varnishing. Use the suds and sanding process (with very fine sandpaper) before applying coats 16 through 20. You will notice, after the 16th coat, that the surface is entirely even and the prints are no longer raised above the rest of the surface.

Step 7

After the 20th coat is dry, mix equal parts of linseed oil and ground pumice to the consistency of honey. Spread the mixture generously on the decoupage surface, using the felt square, and rub the mixture over the entire surface with the felt about 20 times or for about five minutes. The rubbing gives the decoupage a soft, mellow finish. Wipe off the remains of the mixture with a clean cloth or paper towels.

Step 8

Polish lamp base with paste wax.

VARIATIONS

Leta suggests decorating a toilet-seat cover with decoupage to add a fun touch to your bathroom.

Use decoupage to decorate a crib, wooden tray, table or desk top or to make a wall plaque or a paperweight.

FELT FUNHOUSE

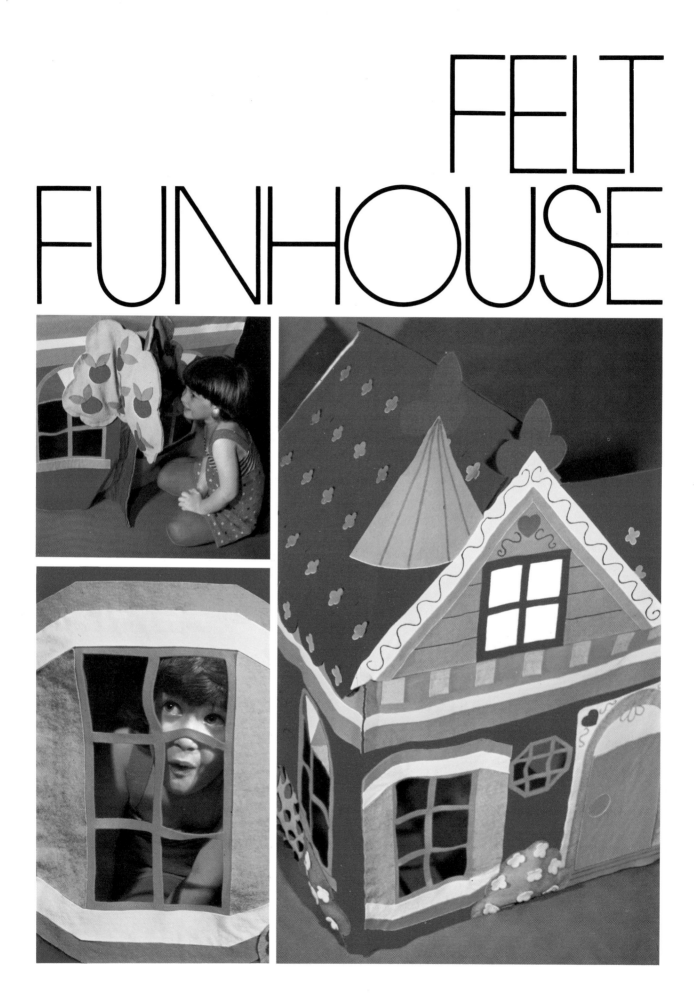

Kathy made this Victorian funhouse, which we designed with some of my favorite San Francisco houses in mind. Sanda loves the colors and shapes, as you can see from the happy-faced picture of her opposite, and Sanda's mother loves the fact that, once the house is removed from its card-table base, it can be folded up and stored in a closet. This project, while not difficult, requires quite a bit of time to complete.

MATERIALS

several large sheets of paper for pattern

pencil and scissors

yardstick

dressmaker's carbon

3½ yds. magenta felt; ½ yd. each green and orange felt; ¼ yd. each yellow, red, turquoise, brown felt

several yds. of cardboard in large sheets about ⅛" thick[20] or smaller pieces taped together; the sides of a large cardboard carton would be perfect

white glue

pins and needle and thread

1 package of polyester or cotton pillow stuffing[17]

30" piece of ½" elastic

2 large hooks and eyes

30" × 30" × 27" card table (if you use a different size table, adjust the patterns)

METHOD

Step 1

Using the instructions on page 150, enlarge the patterns on page 164 to full size on paper. Using dressmaker's carbon, transfer the pattern shapes to cardboard or the appropriate colors of felt as indicated on patterns and cut out. (Use photograph as color guide.)

Step 2

Work on one side of the house at a time, carefully cutting out windows and gluing on smaller pieces to the magenta main body of the house.

Step 3

The front and back roof façade pieces of the house require a cardboard backing. Place these sections of the front and back on the cardboard and trace around edge with pencil. Cut out cardboard ¼" in from the edge so that it is slightly smaller than the house pieces. Glue cardboard to the wrong side of the felt, cut another piece of felt to cover the other side of cardboard and glue.

Step 4

Using photograph and patterns as a guide, glue small pieces of felt—i.e., the shingles, windows and decorative details—to the roof façade. Sew a large eye on the back of each of the two façade pieces where indicated on the pattern.

Step 5

Cut a 30" square of magenta felt and with right sides together stitch two of its edges to the two sides of the house on a ¼" seam allowance, as shown in fig. 1. Stitch three of the four walls of the house together with a ¼" outside seam (wrong sides together). The open corner will serve as the entrance to the house. Place house on card table.

Step 6

On fold lines, fold the cardboard that is the base of the peaked roof. Glue on the magenta piece that covers this cardboard. Then glue shingles and medallions to felt. Place roof in position on top of house. Fold and sew both ends of a 30" piece of elastic under ¾" and attach a hook to each end. Attach one hook to the eye on one of the roof façade pieces, run the elastic through the triangle formed by the peaked roof and attach the other hook to the opposite façade eye. (See fig. 2.)

Step 7

Make the apple tree. Glue leaves at random to right sides of tree tops and pin until dry. Glue around half of the circumference of each apple, attach to tree, slip some stuffing under apple (see fig. 3) and glue around the rest of the circumference. Pin until glue is dry and remove pins. Glue half of the outside edges of the top of one of the trees in the same manner, add stuffing, glue rest of tree tops and pin until dry. Repeat for the top of other tree. Insert cardboard backing between felt sides of tree trunk and glue. Repeat for other tree trunk. Place finished trees face down and on wrong side glue the right half of one tree trunk and the left half of the other. (See fig. 4.) Press these glued areas together and pin until dry. Fold joined trees open and glue wrong side of trees to house. Pin until dry.

Step 8

Glue bushes to house in the same manner as you glued apples to tree, puffing them out with a little stuffing. Pin to dry. You now have finished a house that will delight any child.

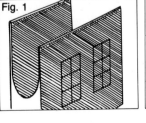
Fig. 1

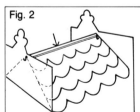
Fig. 2

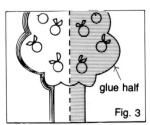
glue half
Fig. 3

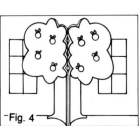
Fig. 4

CREWEL LETTERS

Use these whimsical Crewel Letters as a guide for stitching a wall hanging with your favorite saying or for initialing a shirt, place mat or pillow.

MATERIALS

tracing paper

pencil

dressmaker's carbon

item to be stitched

embroidery hoop

crewel yarn, 1 small skein in each of your favorite colors

needle

scissors

METHOD

Step 1

Select the saying or initials you wish to stitch. Using tracing paper, trace letters on page 166 and with dressmaker's carbon transfer to fabric. Stretch fabric in an embroidery hoop for the best results.

Step 2

Do an outline stitch along the traced lines. (See embroidery glossary on page 153.) Stitch internal designs as indicated in the pattern on page 166.

Step 3

If you wish, fill in the background area around your saying or initials with satin stitch.

VARIATIONS

Experiment with other stitches for different effects, using the embroidery glossary.

Use the enlarging instructions on page 150 and make giant initials on large objects, such as a denim tote.

BEAN'D BOXES

Red beans, black beans, white beans, spotted beans—all can be found on Bean'd Boxes. Children will love working on the boxes, and so will you. They are so easy to make and will hardly dent your pocketbook. Bean a box today!

MATERIALS

tracing paper

pencil

light-colored dressmaker's carbon

several wooden boxes of various sizes (from hobby shops)

white glue

sponge or clean cloth

assorted beans such as small black beans, red beans, pinto beans, kidney beans, white beans, lentils

clear acrylic spray

METHOD

Step 1

Using tracing paper, trace diagrams on this page to use as a guide for bean arrangement. Adjust diagrams to fit boxes if necessary. Transfer design by placing dressmaker's carbon face down on top of box with traced designs on top of the carbon paper. Trace lines with pencil.

Step 2

After designs are transferred to boxes, apply a thick line of glue on the outlines of the designs. Place beans along the glued line in any combination you find pleasing. Fill in outline with glue and, using the photograph as a guide, arrange beans in pleasing color arrangements until entire design surface is covered. Remove excess glue with wet sponge or damp cloth while the glue is still wet.

Step 3

After the glue has dried completely, spray with several coats of clear acrylic to protect the finish.

VARIATIONS

Trace your initials on the box and fill in with beans that will contrast with those used for the background.

enlarge twice (see page 150)

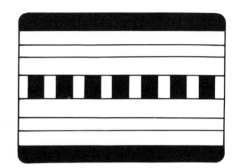

49

BUTTERFLY PILLOW

Add a burst of color to your sofa or bed with this rainbow-hued Butterfly Pillow. Needlepoint is excellent pickup work. Make the butterfly while traveling, commuting or watching TV, and it will be finished in no time at all. Then reward yourself for your good work by having a professional upholsterer or pillowmaker block, back and stuff the needlepoint to give it the perfect finish. It may be expensive to have the pillow finished professionally, but I think it's well worth the cost.

MATERIALS

16″ × 17″ piece of single-mesh canvas[1], 9 to 10 threads to the inch

light-colored permanent marker

masking tape

needlepoint or tapestry needle[1]

1 skein each needlepoint yarn[1] in dark blue-green, medium blue-green, tangerine, fuchsia, Kelly green and primary yellow

several skeins of black embroidery yarn[1] for background

METHOD

Step 1

Place canvas over enlarged pattern and trace pattern to canvas with light-colored permanent marker.

Step 2

Tape the edges of the canvas to prevent its fraying.

Step 3

Using the pattern and photograph as color guides, fill in the butterfly shape with the Continental or basketweave stitch. (See needlepoint glossary on page 150.) Each of the stripes on the butterfly's wings should be about four stitches wide.

Step 4

Fill in the background with black in either the Continental or basketweave stitch.

Step 5

Follow my introductory suggestion and have the pillow finished by a professional or turn to page 151 for blocking, backing and stuffing instructions.

VARIATIONS

Using the instructions on page 150, enlarge the pattern and make a gros-point rug, or, following the instructions on the same page, reduce the pattern and make a petit-point eyeglass or makeup case with a butterfly motif.

Needlepoint the butterfly shape only, cut around the edges of the needlepoint and make a butterfly-shaped pillow.

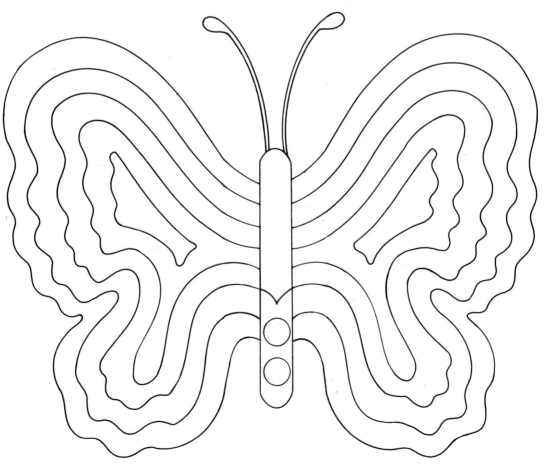

DECO ETCHING

Etching turns an ordinary object, such as a glass or mirror, into a thing of distinction. Etching a monogram or simple design on such objects gives them a classic look. There are three methods for etching: masking with asphaltum, cutting a stencil from wide, smooth tape and using a combination of press-on letters and tape for a negative initial. All methods are surprisingly easy and take very little time.

MATERIALS

pencil (Method I)

carbon paper (Method I)

cellophane tape (Method I)

glasses or mirrors to be etched

½″ flat brush

etching cream[8]

paintbrush (Method I)

asphaltum[21] (Method I)

benzine[21] (Method I)

smooth, wide tape, e.g. Mystic tape (Methods II & III)

wax paper (Method II)

drawing board, cutting board or heavy cardboard (Method II)

X-acto knife (Method II)

press-on letters[2] (Method III)

timer or watch

METHOD I—Etching by Masking

Step 1

Draw the pattern for your design, initial or motif on a piece of paper. Select something very simple for your first etching attempts or use the pattern on page 169 for an art deco design.

Step 2

Slip the paper pattern inside the glass and tape into position. On outside of glass paint the surrounding area not to be etched with a thin coat of black asphaltum and let dry. Apply a second coat. (See fig. 1.)

Step 3

Apply a thick coat of etching cream on the area to be etched, wait two minutes and wash off under running water.*

Step 4

Remove asphaltum with benzine.

METHOD II—Etching by Stencil

Step 1

Trace design onto wide tape that has been rolled out on wax paper. Place on drawing board, cutting board or heavy cardboard.

Step 2

Cut out area to be etched with an X-acto knife. Remove wax paper, position tape on glass and press down firmly, paying particular attention to the corners. (See fig. 2.)

Step 3

Apply etching cream on the area to be etched, wait two minutes and wash off under running water. Peel off tape.*

METHOD III—Etching with Press-on Letters

Step 1

Position letter on glass, transfer to glass by rubbing with a smooth object.

Step 2

Carefully place four strips of tape in a square around the initial. (See fig. 3.)

Step 3

Apply etching cream on the area to be etched, wait two minutes and wash off under running water. Remove letter and tape.*

VARIATIONS

Etch your initials on a decanter.

Make an original set of canisters by etching "flour," "sugar," "tea" and "coffee" on a set of graduated-sized glass jars.

*Brush strokes can ruin the effect of the etching, and although the cream must be brushed on, the application should be made with flowing strokes. Wear rubber gloves when using etching cream. If the cream comes in contact with the skin, rinse immediately with cool, running water.

Fig. 1

Fig. 2

Fig. 3

SWEATER
CRAZYSTITCH

Make a woolly, easy-fitting Crazystitch Sweater and Hat like the ones made by Carla, pictured here. You will learn a whole sampler of stitches. Don't be put off by the length of the instructions. They are really very easy to follow, and the sweater can be finished quickly because of the heavy wool and large needles.

MATERIALS

5 skeins of sheep's wool[1] for sweater

1 pair #11 needles (14″ long) for sweater

box of markers[1] for sweater

cable needle (for bulky wool) for sweater

1 skein of sheep's wool[1] for hat

1 pair #10½ needles for hat

crochet hook or yarn needle

terrycloth bath towel

one box of rustproof pins

METHOD

Step 1

The sweater fits sizes 32 through 36. The gauge is 1″ = 2½ stitches and approximately 4 rows. Make the back. (See knitting instructions, stitches and abbreviations on page 151.) Cast on 50 sts. Work in garter st (knit every row) for 2″, end on wrong side.

Row 1: k 14 sts, place a marker on needle, *k 1, p 1* 6 times—12 sts, place a marker on needle, *p 2, k 1 tbl of st , p 3* repeat from * across remaining 24 sts.

Row 2: *k 3, p 1 tbl of st, k 2* repeat from * to first marker, slip marker, *k 1, p 1*, to next marker, slip marker, p 14.

(From this point on, m = slip marker, and the directions between *s should be repeated until you reach the next marker or the end of a row.)

Row 3: k 14, m, *p 1, k 1*, m, *p 2, k 1 tbl of st, p 3*.

Row 4: *k 3, p 1 tbl of st, k 2*, m, *p 1, k 1*, m, p 14.

Row 5: k 14, m, *k 1, p 1*, m, *p 2, k 1 tbl of st, p 3*.

Row 6: *k 3, p 1 tbl of st, k 2*, m, *k 1, p 1, m, p 14.

Row 7: repeat row 3.

Row 8: p 1 tbl of st, k 5*, m, *p 1, k 1*, m, p 14.

Row 9: k 14, m, *k 1, p 1*, m, *p 5, k 1 tbl of st*.

Row 10: *p 1 tbl of st, k 5*, m, *k 1, p 1*, m, p 14.

Row 11: k 14, m, *p 1, k 1*, m, *p 5, k 1 tbl of st*.

Rows 12 through 15: repeat rows 8, 9, 10 and 11.

Row 16: *p 3 tog (k 1, p 1, k 1) into next st*, m, *p 1, k 1*, m, p 14.

Row 17: k 14, m, *k 1, p 1*, m, p 24.

Row 18: *(k 1, p 1, k 1) in next st, p 3 tog*, m, *k 1, p 1*, m, p 14.

Row 19: k 14, m, *p 1, k 1*, m, p 24.

Rows 20 through 22: repeat rows 16 through 18.

Row 23: *k 2, wl fwd, sl 2 pws, wl bk*, k 2, m, *p 1, k 1*, m, p 24.

Row 24: *p 3 tog (k 1, p 1, k 1) into next st*, m, *p 1, k 1*, m, p 14.

Row 25: wl fwd, sl 1 pws, wl bk, *k 2, wl fwd, sl 2 pws, wl bk *, k 1, m, *k 1, p 1*, m, p 24.

Row 26: repeat row 18.

Row 27: wl fwd, sl 2 pws, wl bk, *k 2, wl fwd, sl 2 pws, wl bk*, m, *p 1, k 1*, m, p 10, place a marker, p 14.

Row 28: *k 2 tog*, m, p 10, m, *p 1, k 1*, m, p 14.

Row 29: wl fwd, sl 3 pws, wl bk, *k 2, wl fwd, sl 2 pws, wl bk*, k 2, wl fwd, sl 1 pws, m, *k 1, p 1*, m, k 10, m, k into f and b of each st. (See fig. 1.)

Fig. 1

Row 30: p 14, m, p 10, m, *k 1, p 1*, m, p 14.

Row 31: *k 2, wl fwd, sl 2 pws, wl bk*, k 2, m, *p 1, k 1*, m, k 10, m, k 14.

Row 32: repeat row 28.

Row 33: wl fwd, sl 1 pws, wl bk, *k 2, wl fwd, sl 2 pws, wl bk*, k 1, m, *k 1, p 1*, m, k 10, m, k into f and b of each st.

Row 34: repeat row 30.

Row 35: wl fwd, sl 2 pws, wl bk, *k 2, wl fwd, sl 2 pws, wl bk*, m, p 3, k 6, p 3, m, k 10, m, k 14.

Row 36: *k 2 tog*, m, p 10, m, k 3, p 6, k 3, m, p 14.

Row 37: k 1, *wl fwd, sl 2 pws, wl bk, k 2*, wl fwd, sl 1 pws, wl bk, m, p 3, k 6, p 3, m, k 10, m; k into f and b of each st.

Row 38: p 14, m, p 10, m, k 3, p 6, k 3, m, p 14.

Row 39: *k 2, wl fwd, sl 2 pws, wl bk*, k 2, m, p 3, sl next 3 sts onto a cable needle and leave at back of work, k 3, k 3 from cable needle (cable made), p 3, m, k 10, k 14.

Row 40: repeat row 36.

Row 41: wl fwd, sl 1 pws, wl bk*, k 2, wl fwd, sl 2 pws, wl bk*, k 1, m, p 3, k 6, p 3, m, k 10, m, k into f and b of each st.

Row 42: repeat row 38.

Row 43: repeat row 35.

Row 44: repeat row 36.

Row 45: *k 1, p 1*, m, p 3, cable over next 6 sts, p 3, m, k 10, m, k into f and b of each st.

Row 46: p 14, m, p 10, m, k 3, p 6, k 3, m, *p 1, k 1*.

Row 47: *k 1, p 1*, m, p 3, k 6, p 3, m, k 10, m, k 14.

Row 48: *k 2 tog*, m, p 10, m, k 3, p 6, k 3, m, *p 1, k 1*.

Row 49: *k 1, p 1*, m, p 3, k 6, p 3, m, k 10, m, k into f and b of each st.

Row 50: p 14, m, p 1, *yo, p 2 tog*, p 1, m, k 3, p 6, k 3, m, *p 1, k 1*.

Row 51: *k 1, p 1*, m, p 3, cable over next 6 sts, p 3, m, k 2, *yo, k 2 tog*, m, p 3, k 8, p 3.

Row 52: k 3, p 8, k 3, m, p 2, *yo, p 2 tog*, m, k 3, p 6, k 3, m, *p 1, k 1*.

Row 53: *k 1, p 1*, m, p 3, k 6, p 3, m, k 1, *yo, k 2 tog*, k 1, m, p 3, k 8, p 3.

Row 54: k 3, p 8, k 3, m, p 1, *yo, p 2 tog*, p 1, m, k 3, p 6, k 3, m, *p 1, k 1*.

Row 55: *k 1, p 1, *m, p 3, k 6, p 3, m, k 2, *yo, k 2 tog*, m, p 3, sl next 2 sts onto cable needle and leave at back of work, k 2, k 2 sts from cable needle, sl the next 2 sts onto cable needle and leave at front of work, k 2, k 2 sts from cable needle (cable made), p 3.

Row 56: k 3, p 8, k 3, m, p 2, *yo, p 2 tog*, m, k 3, p 6, k 3, m, *p 1, k 1*.

Row 57: *k 6, p 2, k 4*, repeat to second marker (put first marker away), end with k 2—26 sts, m, k 1, *yo, k 2 tog*, k 1, m, p 3, k 8, p 3.

Row 58: k 3, p 8, k 3, m, p 1, *yo, p 2 tog*, p 1, m, p 2, *(p 2, k 2) twice, p 4*.

Row 59: *k 2, p 2, k 6, p 2*, k 2, m, k 2, *yo, k 2 tog*, m, p 3, k 8, p 3.

Row 60: k 3, p 8, k 3, m, p 2, *yo, p 2 tog*, m, k 2, *p 10, k 2*.

Row 61: *k 2, p 2, k 6, p 2*, k 2, m, k 1, *yo, k 2 tog*, k 1, m, p 3, cable as on row 55, p 3.

Row 62: repeat row 58.

Row 63: *k 6, p 2, k 4, *k 2, m, k 2, *yo, k 2 tog*, m, p 3, k 8, p 3.

Row 64: k 3, p 8, k 3, m, p 2, *yo, p 2 tog*, m, p 2, *(p 2, k 2) twice, p 4*.

Row 65: *k 2, p 2, k 6, p 2*, k 2, m, k 1, *yo, k 2 tog, k 1, m, p 3, k 8, p 3.

Row 66: k 3, p 8, k 3, m, p 1, *yo, p 2 tog*, p 1, m, k 2, *p 10, k 2*.

Row 67: *k 2, p 2, k 6, p 2*, k 2, m, k 2, *yo, k 2 tog*, m, p 3, cable, p 3.

Row 68: repeat row 64.

Row 69: *k 6, p 2, k 4*, k 2, m, k 1, *yo, k 2 tog*, k 1, m, p 3, k 8, p 3.

Rows 70 through 73: repeat rows 58, 59, 60 and 61.

Row 74: k 3, p 8, k 3, m, k 22 removing marker, place marker, k 14.

Row 75: k 14, m, k 22, m, p 3, k 8, p 3.

Row 76: k 3, p 8, k 3, m, k 22, m, p 14.

Row 77: *sl next 2 sts onto cable needle and leave at back of work, k 2, k 2 sts from cable needle, k 3*, m, k 22, m, p 3, k 8, p 3.

Row 78: repeat row 76.

Row 79: k 14, m, k 3, slip these sts to st holder. Bind off 16 sts, k 2, m (you should have 3 k to right of marker), p 3, cable, p 3.

Row 80: k 3, p 8, k 3, m, k 3.

Row 81: k 3, m, p 3, k 8, p 3.

Rows 82 through 84: repeat rows 80, 81 and 80.

Row 85: k 3, m, p 3, cable, p 3.

Rows 86 through 91: repeat rows 80, 81, 82, 83, 84 and 85 one time.

Row 92: repeat row 80.

Row 93: repeat row 81.

Slip these sts onto a piece of string.

Step 2

Shape the left shoulder. Slip stitches from holder onto needle with needle point ending at neck edge. Attach yarn.

Row 1: k 3, p 14.

Row 2: *k 2, sl next 2 sts to cable needle and leave at front of work, k 2, k 2 sts from cable needle, k 1*, m, k 3.

Row 3: repeat row 1.

Row 4: k 14, m, k 3.

Row 5: repeat row 1.

Row 6: *sl next 2 sts to cable needle and leave at back of work, k 2, k 2 sts from cable needle, k 3*, m, k 3.

Rows 7 through 13: repeat the following rows: 1, 4, 1, 2, 1, 4, 1.

Slip these sts onto a piece of string.

Step 3

Make the front of the sweater following the instructions for the back.

Step 4

Make the right sleeve. Cast on 44 sts and work in garter st for 2″, ending on the wrong side.

Row 1: k 1, *p 2, k 2, p 2*, k 1.

Row 2: p 1, *k 2, p 2, k 2*, p 1.

Rows 3 and 4: repeat rows 1 and 2.

Row 5: k 1, *sl 2 sts to cable needle and leave at back of work, k 1, p 2 from cable needle, sl 1 st onto cable needle and leave at front of work, p 2, k 1 from cable needle*, k 1.

Row 6: p 2, *k 4, p 2*.

Row 7: k 1, *k 1, p 4, k 1*, k 1.

Row 8: p 1, *p 1, k 4, p 1*, p 1.

Row 9: repeat row 7.

Row 10: repeat row 8.

Row 11: k 1, *sl 1 to cable needle and leave at front of work, p 2, k 1 from cable needle, sl 2 onto cable needle and leave at back of work, k 1, p 2 from cable needle*, k 1.

Row 12: repeat row 2.

Rows 13 through 24: repeat rows 1 through 12.

Row 25: repeat row 1.

Row 26: repeat row 2.

Rows 27 through 33: work in stockinette st (knit one row, purl the next, knit the third row, etc.), ending on the right side.

Row 34: k 2, *p 2 (k into f and b of next st) 3 times*, k 2.

Row 35: k 2, *(k 2 tog tbl of st) 3 times, k 2*, k 2.

Row 36: k 2, *p 1 (k into f and b of next st) 3 times, p 1*, k 2.

Row 37: k 2, *k 1 (k 2 tog tbl of st) 3 times, k 1*, k 2.
Row 38: k 2, *(k into f and b of next st) 3 times, p 2*, k 2.
Row 39: k 2, *k 2 (k 2 tog tbl of st) 3 times, k 2*, k 2.
Row 40: k 2, k into f and b of next 2 sts, * p2 (k into f and b of next st) 3 times*, p 2, k into f and b of next st, k 2.
Row 41: k 2, k 2 tog tbl of st, *k 2 (k 2 tog tbl of st) 3 times*, k 2 (k 2 tog tbl of st) 2 times, k 2.
Row 42: k 2, k into f and b of next st, *p 2 (k into f and b of next st) 3 times*, p 2, k into f and b of next 2 sts, k 2.
Row 43: k 2 (k 2 tog tbl of st) 2 times, *k 2 (k 2 tog tbl of st) 3 times, *k 2, k 2 tog tbl of st, k 2.
Rows 44 through 53: repeat rows 34 through 43. Bind off.

Step 5

Make the left sleeve. Cast on 44 sts and work in garter stitch for 2″, ending on the wrong side.
Row 1: k 1, *k 2, p 1*, k 1.
Row 2: k 1, *k 1, p 2*, k 1.
Row 3: repeat row 1.
Row 4: k across.
Rows 5 through 12: repeat rows 1 through 4 two times.
Row 13: k 1, p 1 across.
Row 14: p 1, k 1 across.
Rows 15 through 18: repeat rows 13 and 14 two times.
Row 19: k 4, *k 6, p 1, k 5*, k 4.
Row 20: p 4, *p 4, k 3, p 5*, p 4.
Row 21: k 4, *k 4, p 5, k 3*, k 4.
Row 22: p 4, *p 2, k 7, p 3*, p 4.
Row 23: k 4, *k 2, p 9, k 1*, k 4.
Row 24: p across.
Row 25: k 4, *p 1, k 11*, p 1, k 3.
Row 26: p 2, k 3, *p 9, k 3*, p 3.
Row 27: k 2, p 5, *k 7, p 5*, k 1.
Row 28: *k 7, p 5*, k 7, p 1.
Row 29: *p 9, k 3*, p 8.
Row 30: p across.
Rows 31 through 42: repeat rows 19 through 30.
Rows 43 through 48: repeat rows 19 through 24.
Row 49: p across.
Row 50: k across.
Repeat rows 49 and 50 until piece is the same length as the right sleeve. Bind off.

Step 6

Soak pieces in cool water for 15 minutes. Roll in a terrycloth towel to remove excess moisture and then block to the measurements below on a flat surface with rustproof pins. Front and back pieces: 18″ wide, 24″ long. Sleeves: 16″ wide, 14″ long.

Step 7

Finish the sweater. When the pieces are dry, thread yarn needle with the strand of yarn left attached to shoulder stitches and invisibly graft stitches of front and back shoulder together. Repeat on the other shoulder. Fold bound-off stitches of the sleeve in half and match this to shoulder seam of front and back. Sew sleeve to front and back. Repeat for other sleeve. Sew side seams and weave in any ends of yarn.

Step 8

Make the hat. The gauge for the hat is 3 stitches = 1″. One size fits all. Cast on 68 stitches and work in garter stitch for five ridges, decreasing 2 stitches on the last row.
Row 1: *k 2, p 1*, repeat from * across row.
Row 2: *k 1, p 2*.
Row 3: *k 2, p 1*.
Row 4: k across row.
Rows 5 through 12: repeat rows 1 through 4 two times.
Row 13: k 2 tog, *p 1, k 1*, repeat from * across row.
Row 14: *k 1, p 1*, repeat from * across row.
Row 15: *(k 1, p 1) 11 times, k 2 tog, p 2 tog*, repeat from * 1 time, (k 1, p 1) 5 times, k 1, p 2 tog.
Row 16: *p 1, k 1*.
Row 17: (k 1, p 1) 5 times, k 2 tog, p 2 tog, *(k 1, p 1) 10 times*, k 2 tog, p 2 tog, repeat from * to * ending with k 2 tog—55 sts.
Row 18: *k 1, p 1*, repeat from * across row.
Row 19: k 1, p 1, k 1, p 2 tog, k 2 tog, *(p 1, k 1) 4 times, p 2 tog, k 2 tog*, repeat from * to end of row—45 sts.
Row 20: *(k 1, p 1) 3 times, k 2 tog, p 2 tog*, repeat from * 4 times, (k 1, p 1) 2 times, k 1—37 sts.
Row 21: *k 1, p 1*, end with k 1.
Row 22: k 2 tog, p 2 tog, (k 1, p 1) 2 times, *k 2 tog, p 2 tog, (k 1, p 1) *5 times, k 2 tog, p 2 tog, (k 1, p 1) 4 times, p 2 tog—30 sts.
Row 23: *p 1, k 1*.
Row 24: *p 2 tog, k 2 tog, p 1, k 2 tog, p 2 tog, k 1* across row—18 sts.
Row 25: *k 1, p 1*.
Row 26: *p 2 tog, k 2 tog*.
Break off yarn, leaving a 20-inch end.

Step 9

Finish hat. With a crochet hook or yarn needle, draw end of yarn through remaining stitches and draw up tight. Fasten securely and use remaining yarn to sew seam.

CALICO TRAY

This Calico Tray will create a bright background for whatever you serve, making breakfast in bed or just having a snack in front of the TV an occasion. The "farmscape" is made of calico scraps, which you are bound to have around the house if you've made other projects in this book. Use this design or create some other whimsical scene, like the "Drink Milk" tray shown here.

MATERIALS

tracing paper

pencil

dressmaker's carbon

12½″ × 16½″ rattan or wicker tray[18] with a piece of glass cut to fit into the tray

a piece of paper at least the size of the tray

scissors

pins

several colored scraps of calico

13″ × 17″ piece of blue denim

iron-on fusing tape

iron and ironing board

sewing machine (optional)

bright-colored thread (optional)

rickrack (optional)

embroidery thread and needle (optional)

12½″ × 16½″ piece of lightweight cardboard [2, 20]

masking tape

METHOD

Step 1

Cut a piece of paper to fit your tray. Using tracing paper, trace the pattern on page 168, and with carbon, transfer to paper. Enlarge the design, using the instructions on page 150. Cut along the lines of the design and use the resulting pieces of paper as patterns. Pin patterns to the calico scraps and cut out.

Step 2

Using the photograph as a guide, place the pieces of calico on the 13″ × 17″ piece of blue denim and secure in place by slipping the fusing tape under the adjoining edges of the pieces and pressing with a medium-hot iron.

Step 3

Finish the patchwork by sewing a machine zigzag stitch around the edges of the pieces in contrasting thread or by using an embroidery stitch or bits of rickrack to outline each piece.

Step 4

Trim the cardboard so that it fits into the tray perfectly. Back the calico patchwork with the cardboard and tape the overlapping cloth edges to the back of the cardboard with masking tape.

Step 5

Insert calico patchwork in tray and place glass on top.

VARIATIONS

Create your own design for the calico patchwork. Make one with flowers, animals or some theme that is meaningful to you.

Make a calico scene, frame it and hang in kitchen or bathroom.

CLAY FRAMES

These frames have the look of ceramic but are actually made from self-hardening clay and can be used to frame small photographs, mirrors and paintings. The clay can be found in most art stores or you can make your own from the recipe below. The project is very simple, requiring a minimum of time and equipment. And it's great fun to work with the clay—rather like a return to childhood!

MATERIALS

small 5-lb. box of self-hardening clay[2] or 1 recipe of clay (below)

rolling pin

ruler

tracing paper

straight pin

knife

cookie cutters

paper

1 small jar of paint, such as tempera, acrylic or model-airplane paint[2], in each of your favorite colors (optional)

clear shellac, clear acrylic spray[2] or clear fingernail polish

a piece of stiff cardboard (at least as big as the finished frame)

masking tape

white glue

RECIPE

1 cup cornstarch

2 cups baking soda

saucepan

1¼ cups cold water

damp cloth

Mix cornstarch and baking soda in a saucepan until thoroughly blended. Add water and cook over medium heat for about four minutes, stirring constantly until mixture thickens and has the consistency of moist mashed potatoes. Cover with damp cloth and cool. Knead like dough for about five minutes. Use the dough soon after it is made; it will harden in 8 to 12 hours.

METHOD

Step 1

Mix self-hardening clay according to directions or use cooled and kneaded recipe above. With rolling pin roll out clay to a ¼″ thickness.

Step 2

Make the frames in one of the following ways: (A) Use tracing paper to trace patterns on page 169 and lay over clay. Use a straight pin to transfer the design to clay with a series of pinpricks. Cut out with knife and decorate by pressing designs into the clay. (See fig. 1.) (B) Cut out shapes with a cookie cutter, overlap the edges of the shapes to form lengths and widths (the sides of the frame) and join the strips to form a frame. (See fig. 2.) (C) Take a lump of clay and press it into several narrow strips. Weave the strips together as you would a basket, forming a frame shape. Use the photograph and fig. 3 as guides.

Step 3

Paint the frames with tempera, acrylic or model-airplane paint if you wish.

Step 4

Spray or coat with plastic, shellac or with clear fingernail polish.

Step 5

Mount your picture, mirror or painting. Cut a piece of stiff cardboard to a size slightly smaller than the outside dimensions of the frame. Center the picture, etc., and tape in place with masking tape. Apply white glue to the back of the frame and the edges of the cardboard that will meet the frame. Place frame on cardboard, press firmly and let dry. Cut a stand out of cardboard (See fig. 4) or attach a loop of cord to the back of the cardboard and hang on a wall.

VARIATIONS

Use the clay to make paperweights, jewelry or candlesticks.

Make a frame for a friend's photograph to give as a special gift.

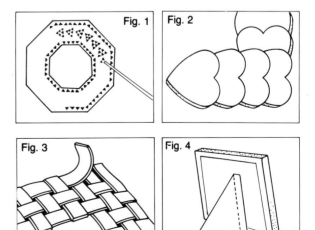

Fig. 1   Fig. 2   Fig. 3   Fig. 4

FANTASY
FLOWERS

Lasting and beautiful, these Fantasy Flowers will add cheer to any room with their happy colors. They are easy to do and are a great way to use up leftover needlepoint yarn.

MATERIALS

1 yd. needlepoint canvas 12 to 14 threads per inch[1] for a medium-size bouquet

light-colored permanent marker

masking tape

1 small skein each needlepoint yarn in yellow, leaf green, cadmium orange, magenta, turquoise, aqua, violet, royal blue, teal blue[1] (if you use Persian yarn, use two strands)

needlepoint needle

handful of cotton or polyester filling

one terrycloth towel

iron

6' of ¼" wooden dowel or 6' of stiff wire, such as that used in wire coat hangers

saw or wire cutters

METHOD

Step 1

Place canvas over patterns on page 170 and trace with a light-colored permanent marker. Trace two of each flower, one for the flower front, the other for the flower back. Bind all edges of canvas with masking tape to prevent raveling.

Step 2

Following pattern color guide, stitch leaves, stems and flowers in the appropriate colors, using a continental or basketweave stitch. (See needle-point glossary.)

Step 3

When stitching is completed, dip canvas in warm water and stretch back to original shape. Place face down on towel and press with a warm iron.

Step 4

Cut out each piece, leaving ¼" seam allowance around all edges. (See fig 1.) Press under seam allowance.

Step 5

With wrong sides together, slipstitch around the edges of all flowers, leaves and stems, leaving the bottom of the stems open for the insertion of dowel or wire and leaving a small opening in flower for filling. Stuff flower lightly with cotton or polyester filling and slipstitch opening closed. (See fig. 2.)

Step 6

Use saw or wire cutters to cut the wooden dowel or wire into pieces that are equal to the length of the stems less the seam allowance. Insert dowel or wire inside stem and slipstitch bottom edge of stem closed.

Step 7

Arrange your flowers in a vase.

VARIATIONS

Needlepoint a vase or basket in which to arrange the Fantasy Flowers.

Needlepoint only one kind of flower or flowers in a single color.

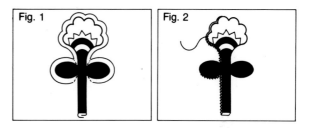

Fig. 1 Fig. 2

FAKE ONYX

This elegant jewelry is made from plastic but has the expensive look of onyx. The project is of medium difficulty; but I think you'll agree that the finished product makes your efforts worthwhile. Best of all, Fake Onyx is inexpensive to produce.

MATERIALS

tracing paper

a piece of paper for pattern

pencil

carbon paper

scissors

1/8" to 1/4" thick black plastic[11]; a 2" × 4" piece will be enough for one pin and one pendant

white grease pencil or straight pin

saber saw[16] or jeweler's saw[3] with metal cutting blades

1 sheet each coarse, medium, fine, very fine open-coat sandpaper

vise or clamp[16]

buffing wheel (optional)

half-round jeweler's file[3] (optional)

hand or electric drill with 1/16" bit

epoxy glue[16]

silver chain or black cord (for pendant)

pin back[3] (for pin)

METHOD

Step 1

Using tracing paper, trace patterns on this page and with carbon paper transfer to paper. Carefully cut out pattern with scissors.

Step 2

Place pattern on plastic and trace outline with grease pencil or with a straight pin. You will need one shape for each pendant or pin.

Step 3

Put plastic in a vise or clamp and carefully saw out shape. (See fig. 1.) Unclamp and sand only the edges with the roughest sandpaper to the finest. If you have access to a buffing wheel, file edges round and buff or take to a jeweler for buffing.

Step 4

For the pendant, drill one 1/16" hole where indicated on the pattern through the upper part of the shape. Do not, of course, drill any holes in the pin.

Step 5

Thread pendant shape on silver chain or black cord. Finish the pin by gluing a purchased pin back to the wrong side of the shape with epoxy glue.

VARIATIONS

Cut out a shape that is meaningful to you.

Cut out plastic shapes of various colors.

String several shapes together and make a long necklace.

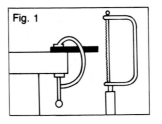

Fig. 1

actual size

BREAD
SCULPTURE

This project for Bread Sculpture was inspired by traditional Greek wedding bread I saw on the island of Crete. A simple doughnut shape was encrusted with roses, flowers, fish, birds and leaves. Sprayed with acrylic, the Bread Sculpture looks great hanging on a wall or used as a centerpiece. Study the photograph and make one of your own.

MATERIALS

1½ cups salt

2¼ cups hot water

6 cups unsifted flour

large bowl

large spoon

floured pastry board or cloth

ungreased cookie sheet

rolling pin

toothpicks or fork

egg yolk

clear acrylic spray

15″ × 1″ strip of leather (optional)

METHOD

Step 1

With a large spoon mix hot water and salt in a bowl until the salt is dissolved. Slowly add the flour and stir until the mixture can be formed into a ball.

Step 2

Place dough on a floured pastry board (or cloth) and knead until smooth and easy to handle. (This takes about six to ten minutes.) You should be able to roll and mold it without its flaking or sticking to the hands. Sparingly add more flour if too sticky or more water if too dry.

Step 3

Use about three-fourths of the dough to mold a large doughnut shape approximately 8″ across and with a 3″ opening. Set aside on an ungreased cookie sheet.

Step 4

Roll out the remaining dough to a ½″ thickness. Using the photograph as a guide, cut out and mold shapes similar to the ones pictured. Make grooves on the shapes with toothpicks or a fork. Attach shapes to the doughnut shape with a mixture of one egg yolk and one tablespoon of water.

Step 5

Bake sculpture 40 to 50 minutes at 300°. Check to see if the sculpture is done by tapping it. It should have a solid sound. If it doesn't, return it to the oven for a few more minutes.

Step 6

When the sculpture is completely cool, spray with clear acrylic. Place the sculpture on a table or tie a piece of leather around it and hang it on a wall.

VARIATIONS

Use this versatile dough to make Christmas ornaments, jewelry or miniature sculptures. The dough can be tinted with food coloring or painted with tempera and then shellacked. Make a Christmas wreath for an interior door.

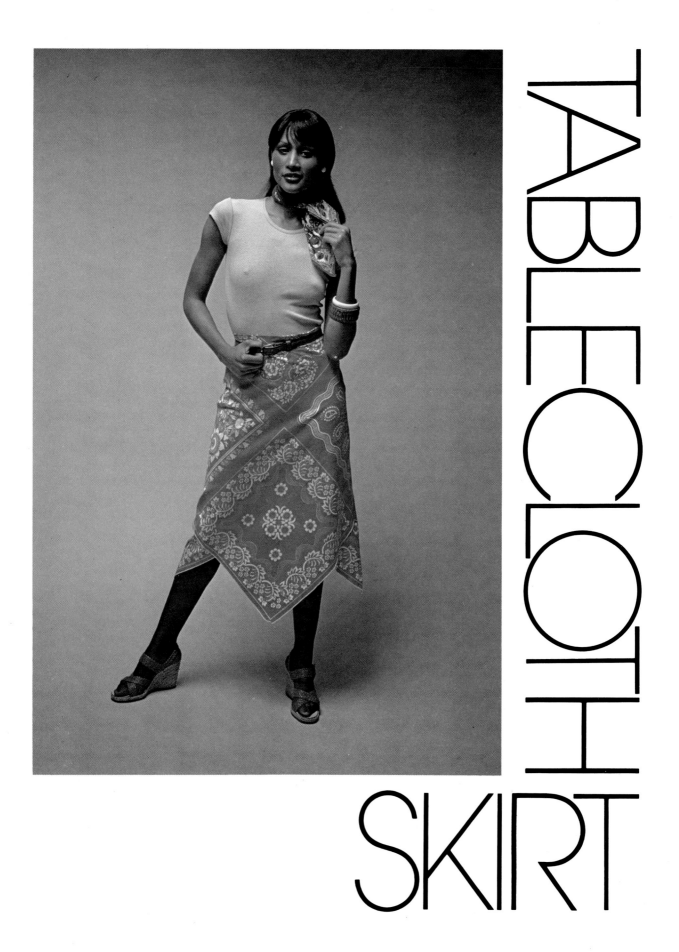

TABLECLOTH
SKIRT

Here is a skirt that, paired with a T-shirt, can serve as your summer uniform. It's pretty, very different and so easy to make. Use a print, solid color or a bordered cloth. Since the tablecloth is already hemmed, your sewing time is kept to a minimum.

MATERIALS

1 tablecloth at least 45″ square or larger.

yardstick

pins

dressmaker's carbon

simple bias A-line 3-piece (front, back, waistband) skirt pattern

scissors

matching thread

sewing machine

7″ skirt zipper in matching color

2 hooks and eyes

METHOD

Step 1

Fold the tablecloth in half on the bias (forming a triangle). Measure 31″ in from both fold tips and mark with pins. (See fig. 1.) This measurement affects the skirt length. If you are very petite, measure 28″ in from the tips. If you are quite tall, measure 33″ in and use a tablecloth larger than 45″ square.

Step 2

Place fold lines of back and front pattern pieces on fold with waist seam lines at the 31″ marks. Pin in place and cut all but the hem edges. (See fig. 2.) Cut an 11″ square (double thickness) using the third point of the triangle as one of the square's corners. Cut waistband. The waistband may have to be pieced, depending on your pattern and the size of your tablecloth.

Step 3

Follow pattern directions for sewing skirt, making sure that the side seams are perfectly even at the hem.

Step 4

Fold skirt (right side out) in half, matching side seams. Slip the unhemmed corners of the 11″ squares under the edges of the skirt so that the points of the squares are on the seam lines of the skirt. The hemmed tips of the corners should fall in a straight line with the tips of the skirt and should form the same length. (See fig. 3.) Pin squares in place and then topstitch close to the edge of the skirt. Press and trim underside of squares to ⅝″ from the topstitching.

VARIATIONS

Vary the length of the skirt. Make it short-short or to the floor.

Use a large tablecloth and make a sundress with an appropriate pattern.

Use the leftover material to make a matching tote bag.

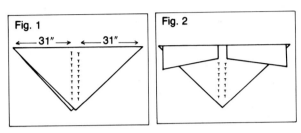

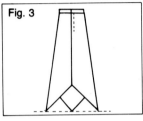

HOT HANDLERS

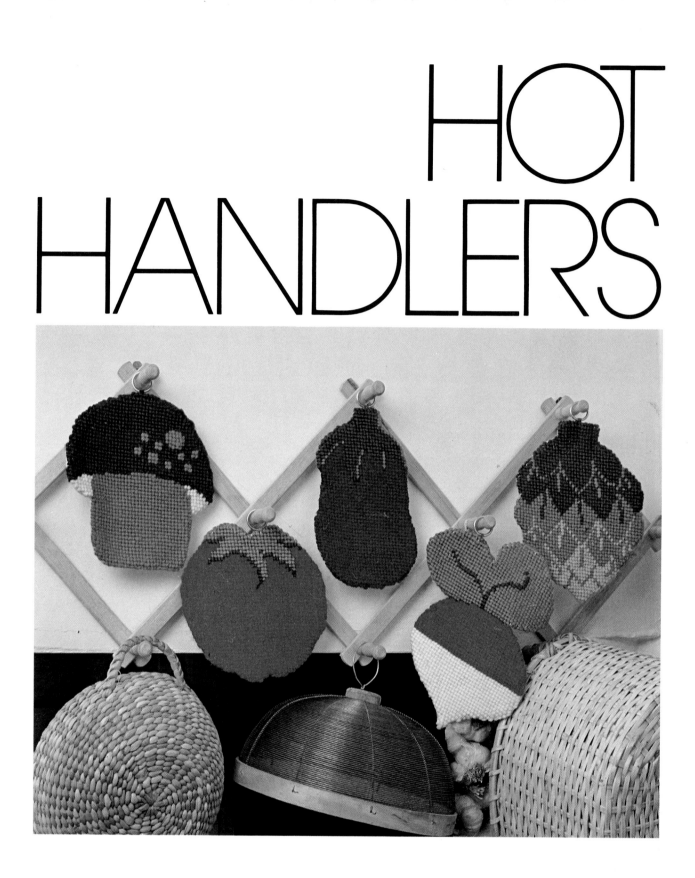

Decorative and practical, these Hot Handlers are the perfect kitchen accessory when grouped attractively and accessibly on a kitchen wall. They are fabric on one side and colorful quick point on the other.

MATERIALS

¼ yd. quick-point canvas[1]

light-colored felt-tip permanent marker

scissors

masking tape

1 skein quick-point yarn in each of the following colors: orange, purple, red, white, tan, magenta, brown, and 1 each of 2 to 3 shades of green[1]

large, blunt needle

terrycloth bath towel

iron

small package quilt filling

¼ yd. cotton fabric for backing in yellow, turquoise or brown[10]

5 brass rings[5]

METHOD

Step 1

Trace patterns on page 158 to canvas by placing canvas over pattern and tracing pattern line with the permanent marker. Cut out of canvas, allowing a ½" seam allowance around all edges. Bind edges with tape to prevent unraveling.

Step 2

Using the patterns and the photograph as guides, stitch the canvas in Continental stitch. (See needle-point glossary on page 150.)

Step 3

Block pieces by dipping them into warm water and stretching back to their original shapes. Place pieces face down on a bath towel and press with a warm iron.

Step 4

Unroll quilt filling on top of the wrong side of the backing fabric. Pin vegetable canvases right side up to filling and backing. Baste around edges and trim.

Step 5

Cut the remaining fabric into bias strips 1" wide and join the strips to form a length of "binding." Fold lengthwise edges under ¼" and press.

Step 6

Starting at the top of the vegetable, pin binding strip over raw edges of the canvas, filling and backing fabric. Baste in place and machine topstitch.

Step 7

Attach rings to top of vegetables. To keep your potholders looking pretty, spray with a stain guard and wash by hand with cold-water soap when necessary.

VARIATIONS

Make a wall hanging. Sketch a pattern for one more vegetable, divide your canvas into six rectangles and stitch a vegetable in each, alternating bright-colored backgrounds.

SHELLINGS

Sea shells are one of nature's works of art. The following project enables you to use these natural masterpieces to create beautiful objects. I used a great number of cowrie shells because of their simple shape and rich colors, ranging from snow white with beige speckles to deepest cocoa with chocolate. In the lamp and basket the cowrie shells are combined with a variety of white and beige shells. This project is easy and inexpensive if you use your beachcombing finds.

MATERIALS

mirror, at least 8″ square (Method I)

cardboard, 13″ × 13″ (Method I)

pencil (Method I)

mat knife (Method I)

masking tape (Method I)

13″ × 13″ square of plywood (Method I)

white glue (Methods I and II)

place mat (as gorgeous as possible) at least 13″ × 13″ (Method I)

masking tape (Method I)

metal-edged ruler (Method I)

approximately 22 cowrie shells [6] (Method I)

clear acrylic spray[19] (Methods I, II, III)

two screw eyes (Method I)

picture wire (Method I)

many shells of various kinds and sizes [6] (Methods II, III)

lamp with clear base (Method II)

basket (of any kind or size)

starfish (optional)

METHOD I—The Mirror
Step 1
Center your piece of mirror on the cardboard, trace the mirror's outline and cut out the traced square as accurately as possible. Fit the mirror in the space and tape securely front and back. (See fig. 1.)
Step 2
Glue mirror and cardboard to plywood.
Step 3
Mark a 13″ square and a 7″ square (centered) on the wrong side of the place mat. Firmly press masking tape ⅛″ away from all cutting lines to prevent unraveling. (See fig. 2.) Use a ruler and mat knife to cut along lines. I find I have more control over the knife when I make several light cuts rather than a single heavy one. Remove cut-out center, check to see that the edges are neat and lightly touch edges with white glue to prevent unraveling. Do the same on the edges of the 13″ × 13″ square.
Step 4
Generously coat wrong side of place mat with white glue and center place mat over mirror (wrong side down on right side of mirror). The place mat is now your mirror's mat.
Step 5
Arrange shells on the mat as I have done in the photograph. Mix colors and sizes to get a natural effect and glue them in place when you are pleased with their appearance. Let the glue dry thoroughly. Cover the mat and mirror with paper and spray shells with clear acrylic spray.

Step 6
Insert two tiny screw eyes in the back of the plywood at opposite sides 1″ from edges and just above center and wire for hanging or glue a triangle of wood to the back of the mirror for a stand. (See fig. 3.)

METHOD II—The Lamp
Step 1
Take lamp apart so that you have access to the interior of the base.
Step 2
Select the shells you wish to use to fill the base and spray them with clear acrylic spray.
Step 3
Arrange the shells in the lamp base so that the best part of each shell faces out. Carefully re-assemble the lamp without disturbing the arrangement of shells.

METHOD III—The Basket

Put the larger or less attractive shells on the bottom of the basket (or use a filler, such as tissue paper, if it will not be seen) and arrange the more interesting shells on top. Glue the shells together and top with a starfish, if you wish. Spray with clear acrylic.

VARIATIONS
Use different combinations of shells or vary the size of the mirror from a small hand mirror to a huge mirror several feet high.

Instead of a mirror, make a frame for your favorite photograph, keeping it simple so that it does not detract from the picture.

Take a short cut by using an old frame or one from the dime store and covering it with shells.

Make an all-white frame by coating the shells with gesso (found in art-supply stores) and then brush on medium acrylic gloss or spray with clear acrylic.

Fill an apothecary jar with shells.

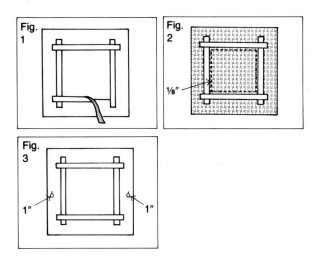

Fig. 1   Fig. 2   ⅛″   Fig. 3   1″   1″

BATIK
SCARVES

Try your hand at the age-old art of batik with these attractive silk scarves. Pure silk takes on the vibrant hues of the dyes perfectly. Andrea, who once taught batik, made the scarves pictured here. I know you will find this batik project as fascinating and as satisfying as we did.

MATERIALS

1 box of push pins[2]

2 white silk scarves 22″ or 23″ square or ⅔ yds. of 45″ wide white silk cut into 22″ or 23″ squares and hemmed

22″ square wooden stretcher frame[2]

several white candles or beeswax or paraffin[2]

double boiler or electric frying pan

thermometer

soft natural charcoal[2] (optional)

medium-size artist's brush[2]

1 can each cerise, cadmium orange, purple and teal cold-water fabric dyes[2] (1 small package of powdered fabric dye may be substituted, but the colors are not as vivid as those produced by cold-water dye)

rubber gloves

clean plastic dishpan

clean old towel

paper towels or newspaper that is at least two weeks old

iron

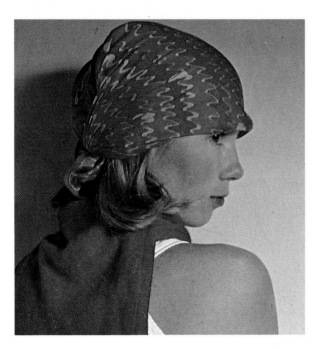

METHOD

Step 1

Stretch the fabric over the wooden stretcher frame, securing the fabric with push pins. Pin one side, stretch the fabric across the frame and pin the opposite side and repeat for the other two sides.

Step 2

Melt the wax in the top of a double boiler or in an electric frying pan (as Andrea does). The wax must be hot enough to penetrate the fabric completely. Begin melting the wax at 350° and then maintain it at about 200°.

Step 3

Charcoal a design lightly on the silk and use a brush to fill in the outlines with wax or simply brush wax over the areas you wish to remain white. Let dry. Remove scarf from frame.

Step 4

You are now ready for the dye. Wear rubber gloves while dyeing to avoid multicolored hands. Mix about ¼ teaspoon of the cold-water dye with two quarts of water in the plastic dishpan. Dip silk square in the lighter color first—i.e., in the pink dye first for the pink and orange scarf, in the blue dye for the blue and purple. Dip the square until the color is of the desired intensity. Rinse in cold water until the water runs clear. Mix the second color.

Step 5

Gently roll the square in a towel to remove the excess moisture and then let dry.

Step 6

Stretch the scarf on the frame once again. Paint with wax the areas that you wish to remain the lighter dyed color and let dry.

Step 7

Dip in the second color following the instructions in steps 4 and 5.

Step 8

Place the scarf between sheets of newspaper or paper towels and press with an iron (hot enough to melt the wax but not hot enough to scorch the silk) until all the wax is absorbed by the paper. Be sure newspaper is at least two weeks old to insure that print won't come off on fabric.

VARIATIONS

Make a shawl for evening with the batik process or batik silk chiffon for an evening caftan.

Frame a batik scarf for an interesting wall decoration.

Use a tjanting tool and batik on cotton for an entirely different look.

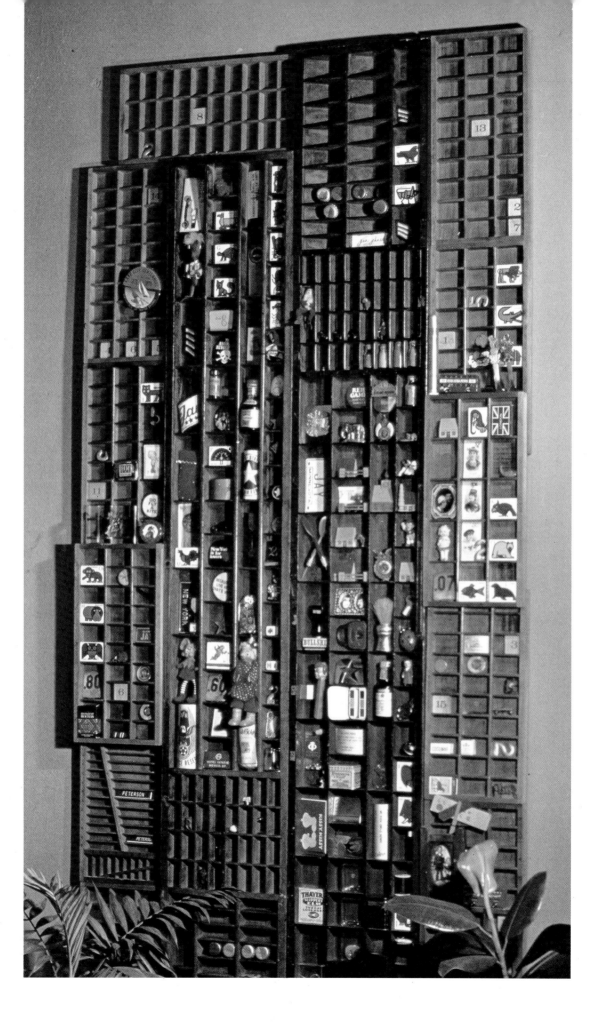

SCRAP BOOK WALL

Jay has come up with the perfect solution to the problem of storing those small items of memorabilia we all like to collect—a Scrapbook Wall. He bought type boxes in a secondhand store, cleaned them, mounted them on a wall and filled them with souvenir match covers, small framed snapshots, a childhood skate key and other goodies. The Scrapbook Wall is intriguing and decorative and it adds a truly personal touch to a room. Search for the type boxes at secondhand stores and junk shops. Use as many as you wish to create a pleasing arrangement.

MATERIALS

an assortment of old type boxes (the kind used on old printing presses)

clear acrylic spray

1½″ flathead screws with plastic plugs (1 for each small box, 2 for each average or large box)

screwdriver

lug bolts (if necessary)

METHOD

Step 1
Wash and clean type boxes, removing the grime but leaving the character. When the boxes are thoroughly dry, spray with clear acrylic.

Step 2
Spread out the boxes before you and plan their arrangement. Note that Jay mounted some boxes (using screws) on the edges of others to create a dramatic effect.

Step 3
Mount the boxes on a wall with screws or with lug bolts, if necessary.

Step 4
Fill the boxes with your collection of memorabilia, arranging colors and shapes for an interesting and pleasing effect.

VARIATIONS

Attach a set of boxes on the wall of a child's room and fill with small toys, cards, rock collections and other child-delighting items.

Use the wall arrangement in the bathroom to hold cosmetics and guest soaps.

TEXAS SHIRT

This rhinestone-studded Texas Shirt, a special favorite of mine, was part of a small collection I did for a well-known boutique in New York City. It looks great with denim or velvet jeans and stands out at any gathering. The process of setting rhinestones is quite simple, but it is rather time-consuming.

MATERIALS

tracing paper

dressmaker's carbon

a satin cowboy-style shirt, any color (either purchased or home-made)

rhinestone setter[19]

#20 rhinestones and backs[19], approximately 100 rose, 475 red, 275 green

METHOD

Step 1

Using tracing paper, trace the design on this page and with dressmaker's carbon transfer to wrong side of the yokes and cuffs. (If you are making the shirt, do this before it is sewn together, leaving space for the seam allowance.) Since the yokes on cowboy shirts vary a great deal, you may have to adjust the design accordingly.

Step 2

Using the rhinestone setter (following the instructions enclosed with the setter), outline all the red flowers first, then fill the outline in with red rhinestones. (See fig. 1.) Next outline the rose tips of the flowers and fill in. Follow same method for the leaves. (You should dry-clean, not wash, your shirt.)

VARIATIONS

Create your own design. Try a desert scene, a cactus arrangement or flamboyant initials.

Take a short cut and just jewel the front yoke of the shirt.

Use sequins instead of rhinestones, sewing them in place with a very fine needle and thread. They are less expensive to use but must also be dry-cleaned with care.

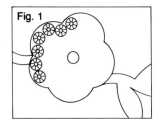

Fig. 1

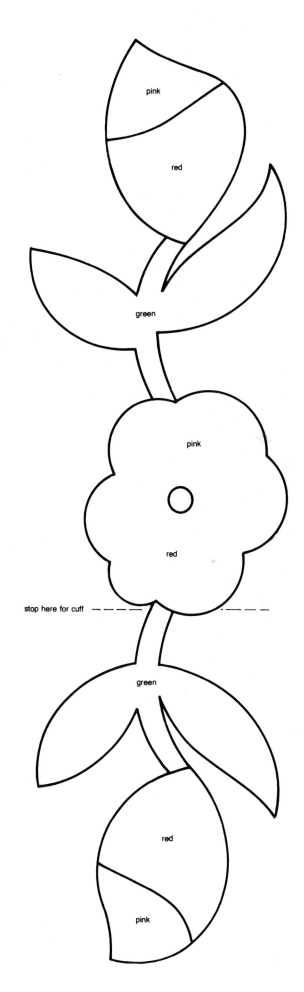

SUPER
SWEATER

You'll finish this Super Sweater in no time at all because it is knitted using five strands of yarn together on extra-large needles. The warm, soft colors create the effect of an impressionistic painting and coordinate beautifully with a broad color range of slacks and skirts. Wrap yourself in this one-of-a-kind sweater and you'll be toasty warm as well as gorgeous!

MATERIALS

twenty-eight 2-oz. skeins of yarn[1]: seven skeins in each of four kinds of yarn (such as sport, mohair blend, bouclés, brushed tweed) in shades of dusty green, teal, rust, peach, several shades of pink, brick, taupe, soft yellow

four 4-oz. skeins of knitting worsted[1] in coordinating colors (e.g., skein dusty green, peach, rust, taupe)

#19 knitting needles (or needles that will give you a gauge of 6 stitches = 4")

size P crochet hook or yarn needle

METHOD
Step 1

For all parts of the sweater use five strands together (one of each kind of yarn) in various colors, changing the colors one at a time (always in the middle of a row) to vary the color combinations of the sweater gradually. One size fits almost all. Knit the back. (See knitting instructions, stitches and abbreviations on page 151.) Cast on 31 sts and k each row until you have reached the desired length to the underarm, approximately 24 ridges on both sides. K 2 tog at the beg and end of every row until 7 sts remain. Bind off loosely.

Step 2

Knit the left front. Cast on 21 sts and k every row until you have the same number of ridges as you had on the back before decreasing. Left front armhole shaping: k 2 tog at the beg of the next row and at end of following row. Repeat last two rows until 9 sts remain.

Step 3

Knit the right front, following the instructions in step 2 but reversing the shaping to the other edge of the piece.

Step 4

Knit the sleeves. Cast on 19 sts and work until the piece measures the desired length from wrist to underarm. Make the same number of ridges on both sides of the pieces. Allow extra length if you want a cuff. K 2 tog at the beg and end of the next row and every other row 6 times until 5 sts remain. K one row and bind off loosely.

Step 5

Knit pockets. (Make two.) Cast on 10 sts and work in garter stitch (all k rows) for 8 ridges. Bind off.

Step 6

Knit belt. Cast on 81 sts and work in garter stitch for 3 ridges. Bind off loosely.

Step 7

Knit the hood. Right side: cast on 1 st. 1st row: inc 1 st. 2nd row: k across. 3rd row: place a marker at the beg of this row (it will be the front of the hood) and inc 1 st. Repeat rows 2 and 3 until there are 8 sts, ending at back of hood. Next row: (back) inc 1 st in the first st and k across. Repeat last row (which will give you an inc on the front of the hood). Repeat last 2 rows until there are 16 sts on needle. Mark last inc row. Work even on 16 sts for 18 ridges. Next three rows: decrease at back edge 3 times (once in each row). K one row even. Place marker for top of hood. Left side: inc 1 st at the back edge for the next 3 rows. Work even until same length as right side. Decrease 1 st at the beg of next 8 rows, ending at the front edge (with 8 sts remaining). Decrease 1 st at the beg of every other row (on front edge) until 1 st remains. Bind off.

Step 8

Join the sweater pieces. Sew sleeves to front and back with flat overcast stitch or crochet them together. Join side and sleeve seams. Join back edges of hood. Join front decreased edge of hood to back of neck, to tops of sleeves and to bound-off stitches of the front. Sew pockets to fronts 2" above lower edges and 2" in from side seams. If you wish, work one row of single crochet (using all five strands of yarn) around outer edge of sweater, sleeves and belt, taking care to keep the work flat.

VARIATIONS

Use the five-strand technique to knit a scarf or mittens, using a simple pattern that requires large needles.

STAMPERS

Stamp your letter envelopes with personalized designs that you have carved in linoleum. The stamps you make will decorate your correspondence in an individual way.

MATERIALS

medium sandpaper
1' of 1" wooden dowel cut in 2¼" pieces[21]
tracing paper
pencil
carbon paper
5" × 7" linoleum block (approx.)[2]
lino cutting tools with fine and medium tips[2]
hand or electric saw
epoxy glue[2]
clear lacquer or spray paint[2] (optional)
stamp pad

METHOD

Step 1
Sand ends of dowels until smooth. Set aside.

Step 2
Using tracing paper, carefully trace designs on this page to paper. Using carbon paper, transfer designs from paper to linoleum block.

Step 3
Using a fine tip on your carving tool, carve around both sides of the lines so that your design is clearly in relief. Always carve away from you and hold block steady. Several light strokes are usually more accurate than one heavy one. Use a medium tip to cut away background.

Step 4
When designs are completely carved, saw blocks apart.

Step 5
Glue a piece of dowel to the back of each block for a handle. Let dry. Lacquer or paint dowel, if you wish, and let dry. You're ready to stamp!

VARIATIONS

Make some designs of your own. Try carving a business card or seasonal motifs for cards and letters.

BARGELLO RUG

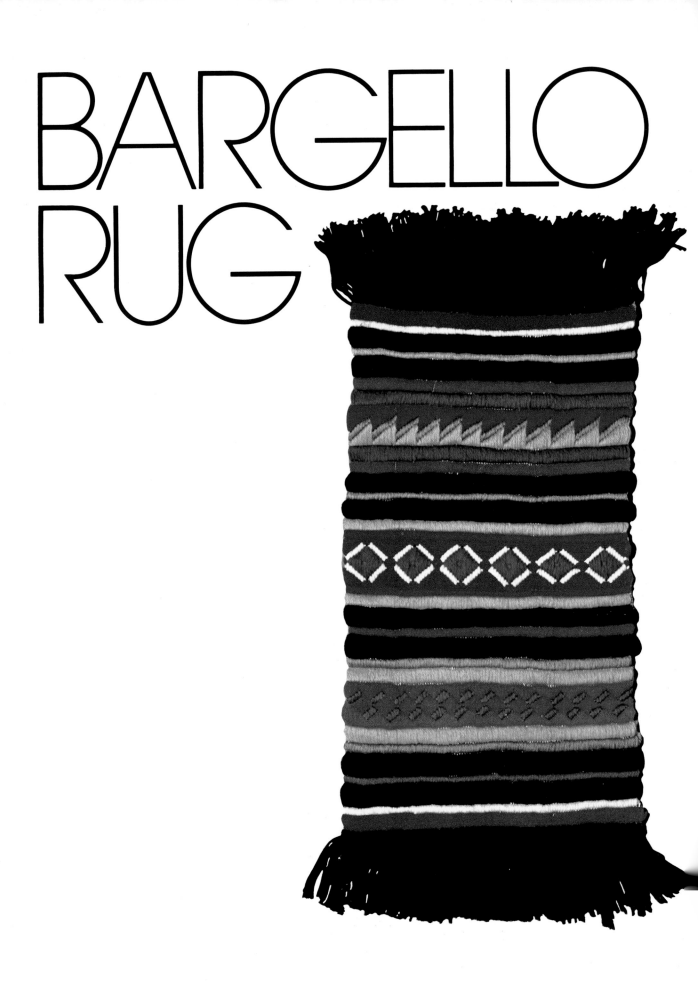

Bargello is a type of canvas work done in vertical stitches by counting threads. It goes so quickly that projects seem to be finished in no time at all. This colorful Bargello Rug is particularly effective in a kitchen or any small room. The design was inspired by a beautiful Mexican patchwork skirt made of hundreds of tiny pieces of bright-colored fabric. As in the skirt, the bright colors of the rug are given impact by the presence of black in the design.

MATERIALS

masking tape

⅝ yd. of 40" wide large mesh canvas (7 squares to the inch)[1]

large quick-point yarn: approx. 6 skeins black; 3 skeins each magenta, red, yellow; 2 skeins each turquoise, green, white[1]

large blunt needle

iron

black carpet thread

rug binding or material for lining (such as canvas) the size of rug plus 1" seam allowance on all edges

crochet hook, the larger the better

METHOD

Step 1

Use design on page 159 for your guide. Each square of the pattern represents one square of the canvas. The yarn is used double in thickness in order to cover the canvas completely. If you use thicker yarn or smaller mesh canvas, however, you may be able to use a single strand of yarn. Bind all raw edges of the canvas with masking tape. The selvage edges will form the top and bottom of the rug and will be fringed.

Step 2

Allowing a 2" margin at raw edges of the canvas, center the middle row of diamonds on the length of the canvas and do a few stitches. Do this to each pattern row on either side of the diamond row and continue to selvage edge to "transcribe" the design to the canvas. Then complete each row. It might be helpful to roll the canvas as you work. Secure the ends of the yarn by weaving through a few stitches on the back of the work. If you make a mistake, pull out the stitch with a needle. Never use scissors, for you might cut the canvas.

Step 3

After the stitching is finished place face down on a damp towel and press with a warm iron.

Step 4

Trim the margin of the canvas to 1", fold back and baste. Miter the corners and baste to the back of the rug.

Step 5

Finish the rug in one of the following three ways. (A) Use rug binding. Pin rug binding on the wrong side, placing one of the binding edges on the fold of the canvas. Miter the corners. Slipstitch to rug. (B) Line the rug. Cut a piece of sturdy fabric to the same size as the rug plus 1" seam allowance on all sides. Press under the seam allowance and slipstitch to back of rug with carpet thread. (C) Whipstitch edges. Using carpet thread, whipstitch around all sides of rug.

Step 6

Make the fringe. Cut 7" lengths of yarn and fold in half. Insert crochet hook from face of rug through back, hook loop and pull taut. (See fig. 1.) Trim ends evenly.

Step 7

To increase the life of your rug, cut a rug pad slightly smaller than rug and place rug on top.

VARIATIONS

Any part of the design is adaptable to any size canvas. Use a small mesh canvas to make a throw pillow or use the large mesh canvas to make a big floor pillow.

Try petit-point canvas and cotton embroidery thread to make frame covers, watch bands, dog collars or address-book covers.

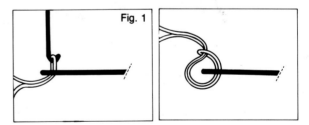

Fig. 1

STAINED
GLASS

The vibrant colors of stained glass are unmatched by anything else. Make this twelve-inch stained-glass square, hang it in your window and add sparkle and warmth to your room.

MATERIALS

tracing paper

pencil

carbon paper

scissors

a piece of paper about 15″ × 15″ for pattern

newspaper

glasses, goggles or sunglasses (to protect eyes)

small pieces of ¼″ glass[12], at least 1″ × 2″ in several shades of brown, red, yellow

glass cutter[2]

small can of kerosene[16]

pliers

felt-tip pen (optional)

one 36-yd. roll of ¼″ wide copper foil tape with adhesive backing[12]

1 small can liquid soldering flux[12]

small, stiff paintbrush

1-lb. spool lead soldering wire[16]

40- to 100-watt soldering iron[16]

one paper clip cut in half

1 small container whiting powder[12]

small, soft paintbrush

soft, clean cloth

METHOD

Step 1

Using tracing paper, trace pattern on next page and with carbon paper transfer to paper and cut out.

Step 2

Cover the working area with newspaper. Be sure to wear glasses, sunglasses or goggles while cutting the glass to protect your eyes from glass dust. I recommend that you practice the cutting and breaking of glass before you begin working on the actual project. Hold the glass cutter as shown in fig. 1, dip cutter in kerosene to make cutting easier and score glass, moving cutter toward you with a firm, steady stroke while holding the glass in place with your free hand. Hold glass firmly with one hand at either side

of the score mark (see fig. 2) and bend it down. Don't be afraid; the glass should snap at score evenly. Any uneven pieces can be nipped away with pliers. After a successful practice session, you are ready to begin.

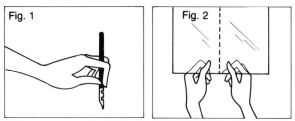

Step 3

Hold the pattern down on the glass with one hand (or mark pattern lines on glass with felt-tip pen), score along cutting line and break, using the method for cutting and breaking outlined in step 2. Always score and break the longest lines first.

Step 4

When all the pieces have been cut out, check to see if they were cut properly by fitting them on the traced pattern. If a piece is not perfect, cut a new one.

Step 5

Wrap the copper foil tape around the edges of each piece. Place the glass edge in the center of the tape (see fig. 3), bend tape over the edges of the glass and press flat with fingers. Overlap the ends of the tape by ¼″ and press firmly in place. (See fig. 4.)

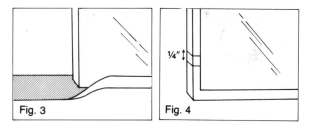

Step 6

After all edges have been taped, place the glass pieces in the pattern shape with edges close together, almost touching. With brush, apply flux to the edges of all the glass sections. Be sure that you work in a well-ventilated area because the fumes from the flux are rather strong.

Step 7

Solder the pieces together. Hold the soldering iron close to the taped edges and touch soldering wire to iron. The solder will melt and drip to connect the taped edges. Spot solder in a few places to hold design together and then steadily solder each seam. If you hold the soldering iron and wire a bit above the seam an attractive rounded, or beaded, seam will be formed. Never hold the soldering iron in one spot more than an instant or your seam will have a lumpy appearance.

Step 8

Solder two halves of the paper clip to the top of the design for hanging.

Step 9

Let solder cool and then use a soft brush to dust whiting powder on solder areas. (It will not harm glass.) Wipe off with soft cloth.

Step 10

Wash stained glass with soap and water so that it will be sparkling clean.

VARIATIONS

Create your own designs for stained-glass decorations. Remember that rectangular or geometric shapes with straight lines are the easiest to work with.

Make a stained-glass frame for a mirror and solder frame to mirror.

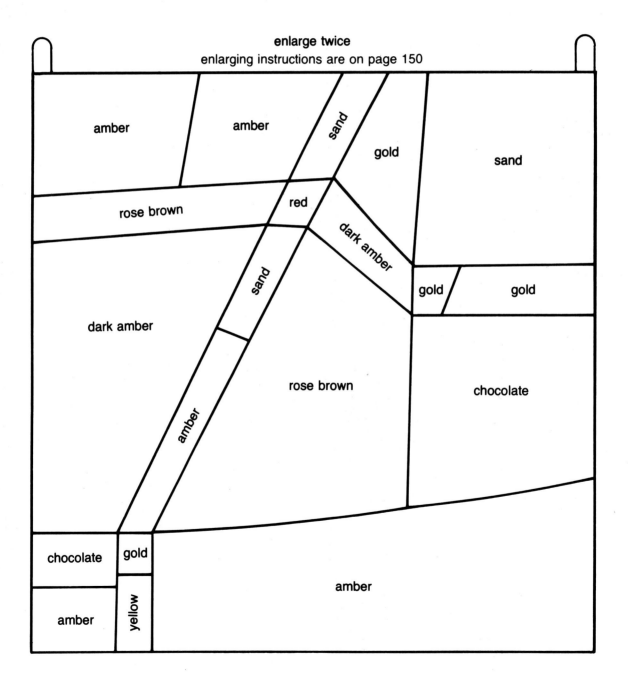

enlarge twice
enlarging instructions are on page 150

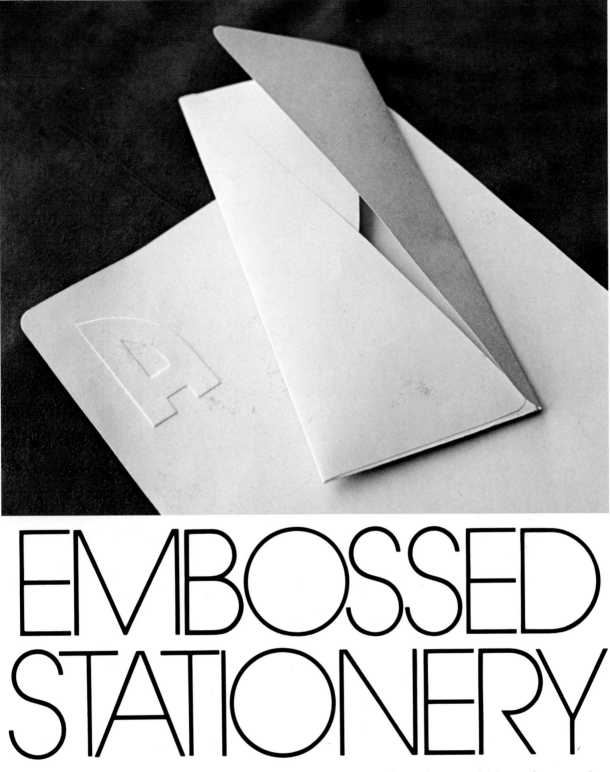

EMBOSSED STATIONERY

A personal letter is a special form of communication. It can convey a mood, a feeling, a personality by its style and by the stationery on which it is written. The following project enables you to express yourself through your stationery as well as through your words, for you may select all the elements—color, weight of paper, style of embossed letter—to create your special message.

Embossing is easy to do and, depending on the paper you select, can become one of the most inexpensive of hobbies.

MATERIALS

paper for stationery and envelopes

a small piece of tracing paper

pencil

dressmaker's carbon

3 pieces of cardboard of the same size, 8″ x 10″ or larger

masking tape

X-acto knife or mat knife

straight edge ruler, T-square, French curve[2] (optional)

rubber cement

hammer

METHOD

Step 1

Choose a paper that has a nice feel to it in a color you like. Remember that color is a key factor in the stationery's effect. Gray, cream or ivory are formal, rich, elegant, while turquoise, yellow or magenta are bright and gay. White is crisp and traditional, and metallic paper is festive and futuristic. I love the effect of brown wrapping paper or even grocery bags. This kind of paper has a natural earth tone, is manageable, and the price is right. Even typewriter paper can be used by those who are inveterate typists. Avoid patterned or highly textured papers or thin, brittle ones such as vellum or tracing paper.

Step 2

Cut the paper to the size you want. A straight edge and X-acto knife work best, and you can cut several sheets at a time. The paper I chose was cut to 8″ x 14″.

Step 3

Choose a letter for embossing. Magazine and newspaper advertisements, shopping bags, shoeboxes, etc., are all sources of simple letter designs. Press-on letters, available in art-supply stores, are the easiest, but for the artist within you, designing your own letter is the most rewarding. If you find a letter you like but it is too large or too small, have it photostated, reduced or enlarged to the size you want, or use the method for reducing or enlarging

given on page 150. Remember that the letter you choose should be simple, with none of the component lines too thin. (Note that the crossbar of the A in the illustration has some width.) Serifs, those small bars at the top and bottom of some letters, are very difficult to emboss and should be avoided. Curved letters are harder to cut than straight ones, but they emboss well—so chin up, all you B, C, D, G, J, O, P, Q, R and S's!

Step 4

Carefully trace your letter on a piece of tracing paper. Place a sheet of carbon paper (dressmaker's carbon is least messy) face down on a piece of cardboard. Center the traced letter perfectly on top, keeping all edges parallel. Tape the edges lightly to hold in place while you trace the initial onto the cardboard. The cardboard should be of medium weight—thick enough to produce an embossing and thin enough to be cut cleanly with an X-acto knife or mat knife. Shirt cardboard or the cardboard on the back of most writing tablets work well.

Step 5

Remove the tracing paper and carbon and use a sharp X-acto knife to cut out the initial. Keep the blade perpendicular to the surface, and cut only on the line. You now have both a positive (the cut-out initial) and a negative (the cardboard from which the initial was cut). Several light cuts are more effective and accurate than a single heavy one. A ruler and a French curve help to keep the lines clean and straight.

Step 6

Use rubber cement to glue the negative face down to another piece of cardboard. (The initial will be backward.) Let the cement dry. Save any small pieces you may have left over, such as the triangular piece from an A, for easier gluing later.

Step 7

Coat the underside of the positive initial with rubber cement and let dry.

Step 8

Place the third piece of cardboard on top of the two that are glued together, making sure that the edges are perfectly even. Tape the three pieces together at the top so that they open and close without slipping (see fig. 1).

Step 9

Open the cardboard sheets and brush rubber cement over the area of the blank piece directly opposite the initial on the negative. Let dry thoroughly.

Step 10

Slip the positive initial face down into the negative, glue the top side of any small pieces of the negative that were left over, insert face down in positive and lower the top piece of cardboard and press firmly over the initial. Lift open, and the positive will be bonded in perfect alignment with the negative. An area coated with dried rubber cement will bond firmly with another such area. Let dry thoroughly.

Step 11

You are now ready to emboss. I suggest making guidelines on the embosser for quicker positioning of the paper and consistency in embossing placement. Open the embosser to the positive. Decide where the left edge of the stationery should be positioned and mark this position on the cardboard (see fig. 2). Using this guideline, slip the paper into position between the pieces of cardboard, close the top and tap initial area lightly with a hammer (or step on it lightly). Open—and you have embossed stationery! It will take a little practice to exert the proper pressure, and your first attempts might come out with rips or creases. To avoid mistakes, use even, light pressure, and you should have clean, lovely embossing.

Step 12

Make the envelopes. Trace the pattern on page 178 to cardboard and cut out. Trace pattern to envelope paper and cut out. Emboss if you wish, then fold in on crease lines in order as follows: A, B, then C. Glue edges lightly, fold down D, and you have an envelope. Write to someone today.

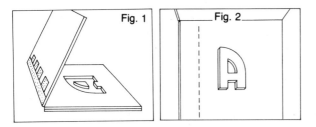

Fig. 1   Fig. 2

VARIATIONS

In addition to stationery, try embossing invitations, notes, seals (purchased or hand-made) and postcards.

Instead of embossing an initial, attempt a simple design, such as a mushroom, a cloud or a heart.

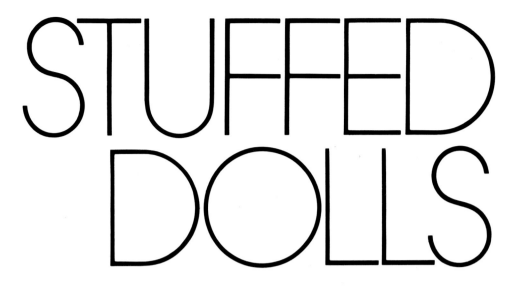

STUFFED DOLLS

Here is a frontier family of Stuffed Dolls, complete with pet cat, for you to make. The dolls, made at very little expense, are cut from muslin, colored with permanent markers, lightly quilted, sewn and stuffed. Creating the frontier family is really a sneaky way to play with dolls again.

MATERIALS

tracing paper

pencil

light-colored dressmaker's carbon

1 yd. muslin 36″ to 45″ wide

1 permanent marker in each of the following colors: purple, turquoise, rust, navy, yellow, red, light green, medium brown

scissors

1 tube of white acrylic paint[2]

1 medium-sized artist's brush

pins

1 small package of quilt filling or batting[17]

sewing machine

needle

2 spools of black thread

1 spool of white thread

1 small bag soft stuffing, such as cotton, kapok or polyester fiber fill[17]

METHOD

Step 1

Using tracing paper, trace the patterns on page 174 and transfer to the right side of the muslin with dressmaker's carbon. Cut out.

Step 2

Using the patterns and photograph as placement and color guides, color the indicated areas. (Experiment on a scrap of material first.) Using artist's brush, paint the little boy's shirt with white acrylic paint. Fill in the other colors with the permanent markers.

Step 3

Pin wrong side of muslin to quilt filling and cut along pattern lines. Baste filling and muslin together along edges.

Step 4

Set your sewing machine for its longest straight stitch and thread with two spools of black thread (if your machine will carry two spools). Topstitch on all lines through muslin and quilting. Leave 1½″ of loose thread at the beginning and end of each stitching line. (See fig. 1.) Bring these loose threads to the wrong side and knot. (The stitching may be done by hand, if you prefer, using the back stitch. See embroidery glossary on page 153.)

Step 5

When all the dolls have been topstitched, place right sides of each doll together and stitch ½″ from all edges with white thread, leaving a small opening for turning.

Step 6

Turn dolls right side out, stuff and slipstitch opening closed.

VARIATIONS

Make large dolls and use as pillows. (See enlarging instructions on page 150.)

Draw a whole family of dolls on one piece of muslin or other fabric, paint, stitch and hang on a wall.

Use felt instead of muslin as the basis for the dolls.

Embroider the details of the dolls instead of coloring them.

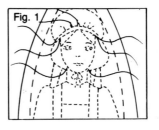

Fig. 1

PARTY NAPKINS

Tie-dyeing is an enormously popular craft because each tie-dyed article is different and always a surprise to unfold. Tie-dyeing is amazingly simple. The napkins can be made from large handkerchiefs or, even better, from old sheets cut into napkin-sized pieces and hemmed. They make a striking buffet decoration stuffed in a basket.

MATERIALS

1 white cotton sheet or 6 large-size cotton handkerchiefs (do not use a polyester blend)

1 package cocoa-brown powdered dye

large pot to dye in

1 bottle liquid dye in each of the following colors: fuchsia, tangerine, cobalt blue and Kelly green

3 plastic bottles with nozzles[17] (such as hair-coloring bottles)

rubber gloves and large spoon for stirring

marbles

wide rubber bands (these will protect lighter areas from the final dye, as well as hold the cloth in gathers, etc.)

METHOD

Step 1

Wash handkerchiefs to remove any sizing. If using a sheet, which I recommend, cut it into six squares, hem by machine and then wash. Tie-dye when cloth is still wet. Prepare brown dye in the large pot according to the package directions. Pour a little of the liquid fuchsia dye into one of the plastic bottles. Do the same with the tangerine. Mix two tablespoons of cobalt blue and two tablespoons of Kelly green and pour into the third bottle. Cap the bottles. The liquid dyes are used undiluted. Wear rubber gloves unless you want tie-dyed hands.

Step 2

Each one of the napkins is tie-dyed in a different manner, using one of the following six methods:

(A) Tied Stripes. Starting at one corner and working toward the corner diagonally opposite, pinch the fabric in small gathers between the thumb and forefinger. (See fig. 1.) Secure these gathers by tightly wrapping the napkin with five rubber bands—three in the center 1½″ apart and one 3″ from each end. (See fig. 2.)

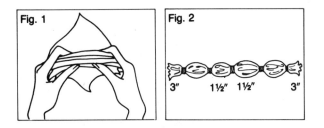

(B) Diamonds. Pour a 3″ circle of fuchsia dye in the center of the square. About ½″ away from the fuchsia circle pour a tangerine circle and about 2″ away from the tangerine pour a circle of blue. (See fig. 3.) Put on rubber gloves and work the dye into the fabric with your fingers to ensure penetration. Pinch center of fabric, lift up and secure with tightly wrapped rubber bands, using fig. 4 as a guide.

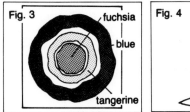

(C) Circles. Pour fuchsia, tangerine and blue dye on the square at random. (See fig. 5.) Pinch up each section and secure with a tightly wrapped rubber band. (See fig. 6.)

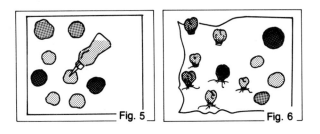

(D) Stripes. Pour a fuchsia stripe diagonally across the fabric from corner to corner. Pour a tangerine and a blue stripe on either side of the fuchsia, leaving a ½″ space in between. (See fig. 7.) Work dye in with fingers. Pinch up in several small gathers and secure with tightly wrapped rubber bands. (See fig. 8.)

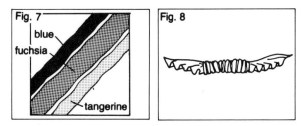

(E) Rounds. Place a marble under the fabric and tightly secure with rubber bands. (See fig. 9.) The napkin in the photograph has a circle in each corner and nine that cross the center.

(F) Multicolored Stripes. Gather the fabric from one edge toward the other and secure with three rubber bands, one at the center and the others 1½″ to the left and right of center band. Secure with two more bands, one 2″ from each side. Pour the tangerine dye in the space between the center band and the

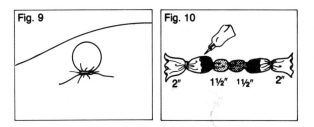

band to its right. Pour the fuchsia in the space between the center band and the band to its left. (See fig. 10.) Pour the blue outside the rubber bands next to the tangerine and fuchsia stripes and completely cover dyed areas with rubber bands.

Step 3

After each napkin is tied, immerse in the brown dye 20 to 30 minutes, stirring continuously.

Step 4

Rinse napkins until the water is fairly clear, untie and continue rinsing until the water runs clear. Let the napkins dry and press. (Remember, the napkins should be laundered separately.)

VARIATIONS

Tie-dye scraps of material and piece into patchwork or make into potholders or place mats.

Have a tie-dye party. It's great fun to tie-dye with a group of friends!

WEDDING SAMPLER

A wedding present should be a personal, lasting expression of your good wishes. The following project enables you to give a gift that is timeless, warm and individual. I got the idea for the project from the sampler collection of my friend Mary Randolph. When she and Howard decided to marry, I wanted to create a special present just for them. You can do the same for your friends by duplicating their eye and hair color, and the color and style of their wedding clothes. The project is time-consuming but inexpensive and well worth the effort.

MATERIALS

lucite frame

1 yd. decorative ribbon for edging

cardboard for mat

a piece of double thread canvas[1] (also called Penelope canvas) as large as your frame

tracing paper

pencil

paper

carbon paper

embroidery needle

light-colored felt-tip permanent marker

1 skein cotton embroidery thread in each of the following colors: rose, peach, yellow, spring green, aqua, lavender, white[1]

1 skein each of cotton embroidery thread for skin tone, hair color, eye color; 3 skeins each of dress and suit colors; 7 skeins of rosy pink for background; 4 skeins dark rose for lettering[1]

cold-water soap

iron

terrycloth bath towels

scissors

white glue

½ yd. backing fabric (white cotton, etc.)

velvet, 1″ larger on all sides than the cardboard mat

METHOD

Step 1

Decide on the size frame, the width of your mat and the width of your ribbon. These will affect the working area of your canvas.

Step 2

Using tracing paper, trace over the photograph and with carbon paper transfer to paper for a guide. (Remember that the pattern size will have to be enlarged or reduced according to the size of your frame, mat and ribbon.) Correct details so that the pattern resembles your bride and groom in their wedding attire.

Step 3

Trace final pattern onto canvas with permanent marker.

Step 4

Stitch your design. Check embroidery glossary on page 153 for stitch instructions. For very tiny details use one or two strands of thread and tiny surface stitches (on top of other stitches). For fine details, such as the faces, feet, hands, shirt, tie and lettering, use three strands of thread and a petit-point stitch. Six strands of thread should be used for the rest. Use a cross stitch for the dress, needlepoint Continental stitch for the background, loose French knots for the bouquet and tight French knots for the boutonniere and edge of the veil.

Step 5

After all the stitching is done, hand-wash canvas with cold-water soap. This will make all white and light colors become bright. Roll canvas in towel and squeeze out excess water. Stretch canvas to original shape, place face down on a towel and press with a warm iron.

Step 6

Sew canvas to cotton backing and turn backing so that it is ½″ larger on all sides than canvas. Glue or sew ribbon around canvas to serve as an edging, making neat mitered corners and hiding ribbon ends under one of those corners (See fig. 1.) Let dry and press lightly if necessary.

Step 7

Place mat on wrong side of velvet, trace along both inside and outside edges with a pencil. Remove mat and trace a one-inch border around mat outline. Cut out and slash into corners. (See fig. 2.) Coat one side of mat with white glue, press glued side down on wrong side of velvet. Fold over border edges and glue lightly. Let dry.

Step 8

Glue mat to canvas, let dry and then slip into frame.

VARIATIONS

Make samplers for other important occasions, such as the birth of a baby.

Cover a dime-store frame with ribbon or material for a different effect.

Use silk thread for your sampler. It is expensive and harder to work with but produces a beautiful, soft look.

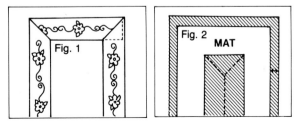

STRAW BERRY PLATES

Give a festive, summery look to your table settings with the following project. Strawberry Plates are pretty, inexpensive and easy to make. You'll need clear glass plates from the dime store, paint and a couple of hours for fun. The paint is made for use on glass and has the look of watercolor. I especially like to use my Strawberry Plates as dessert dishes; they themselves look good enough to eat.

MATERIALS

carbon paper

paper

pencil

clear glass plates

one jar each of yellow, red and Kelly green paint for glass[2]

paint thinner

medium-size artist's brush

METHOD

Step 1

With carbon paper and pencil, trace the pattern on this page to paper.

Step 2

Turn the clean plate upside down over the pattern. The pattern is visible through the clear glass and will serve as a guide while you apply the paint. Paint the strawberries first, then the leaves and the flowers. The best results are achieved if you use your brush with a flowing motion rather than with short, distinct strokes. (The plates must be washed by hand, not in a dishwasher.)

VARIATIONS

Paint a different fruit or flower on each plate or use only white paint for your design.

Because the plates are clear, they show off your table linen. Use place mats or tablecloth in colors that coordinate or contrast with your Strawberry Plates for a striking table arrangement.

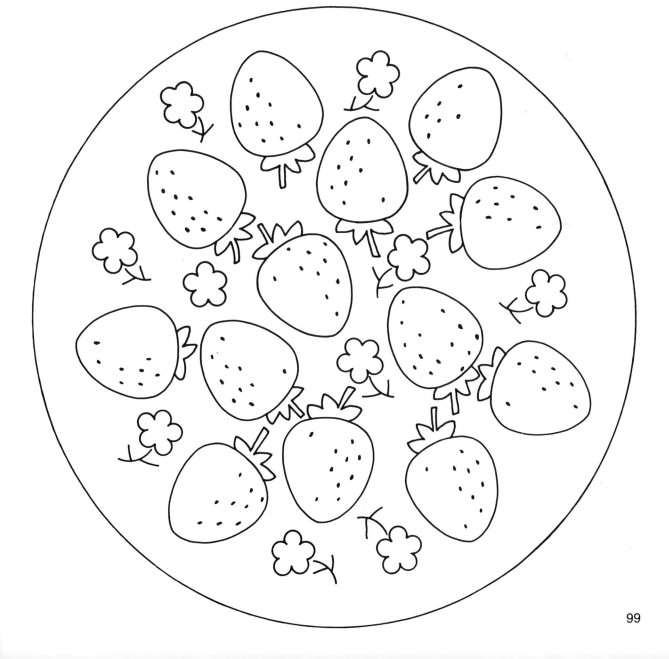

PARTY PINAFORE

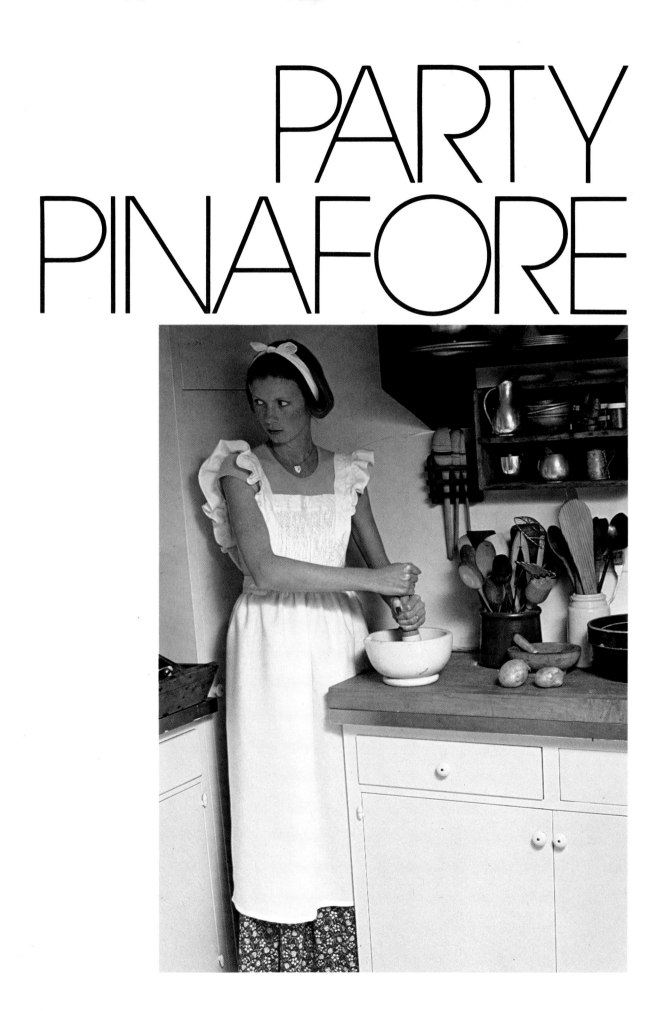

The kitchen will probably be the last place you'll wear this pinafore apron. The hand smocking and white-on-white embroidery give this grown-up Party Pinafore an innocent prettiness that lends a festive look to even the most simple dress. Make a Party Pinafore to keep for yourself or to give as an exceptional gift.

MATERIALS

a few large pieces of paper taped together for pattern, at least 55″ × 30″

pencil and ruler

scissors and pins

2¼″ yds. 45″-wide white cotton broadcloth or lightweight linen[10]

iron and ironing board

8″ × 8″ piece of ½″-spaced transfer dots for smocking or pale-blue tailor's chalk and a clear plastic

1 spool of blue mercerized cotton thread

sewing needle

3 skeins #5 pearl-white embroidery cotton[1]

embroidery needle

white mercerized cotton thread

sewing machine

METHOD

Step 1

Use the instructions on page 150 and enlarge the pattern on page 159 on paper. Cut out pattern pieces, pin to fabric and cut out.

Step 2

Iron the transfer dots to the wrong side of the pinafore bodice (placement marked on pattern). If transfer dots are not available, use tailor's chalk and a clear plastic ruler to mark dots at ¼″ intervals, starting ⅝″ from fabric edges.

Step 3

Starting at the right side of the bodice and working on the wrong side, knot a length of blue thread (which should be removed after smocking) and pick up the first dot. Work across, picking up every dot, and leave 2″ of unknotted thread at the end of the row. Repeat until all rows are finished. Pull the ends of the threads evenly until the piece measures 6½″ across, excluding seam allowance. Knot ends of the gathering threads together, two at a time.

Step 4

Turn bodice to right side and, using embroidery cotton and needle, do five rows of cable stitch on top of blue thread lines. (See embroidery glossary on page 153 .) Next do several rows of smocking stitches, using the stitches that appeal to you. I used six rows of diamond stitch, seven rows of cable, five rows of diamond and five rows of cable to finish.

Step 5

Decorate the sash pieces, bodice strip, straps and shoulder ruffles with the chain, outline or small feather stitch. (See photograph.)

Step 6

Make the sash. Fold both sash pieces lengthwise, right sides together, and stitch around ends, leaving 4″ side openings for turning. Turn right side out, slipstitch openings closed, press and set aside.

Step 7

Hem edges of shoulder ruffles. Turn under edge to be hemmed ¼″ and press. Turn under ¼″ again and hem by hand or machine.

Step 8

Attach ruffles to shoulder straps. Fold straps in half lengthwise, wrong sides together, and press. Prepare the ruffles by stitching two rows of basting between notches. The first row is sewn ½″ from raw edge, the other on seam line. Gather to match notches on shoulder straps and pin. Stitch, press seam toward straps and slipstitch.

Step 9

Sew bodice strip to bodice. (See fig. 1.) Sew right sides together, fold bodice strip over bodice top, turn edge of strip under ⅝″ and neatly slipstitch to wrong side of bodice. Press.

Step 10

Gather skirt on both sides of the bodice to measure 6″ on each side from bodice edge to side edge of skirt.

Step 11

Pin ruffled shoulder straps to both sides of bodice and topstitch together.

Step 12

Pin sash pieces in place on both sides of bodice (see fig. 2) and topstitch.

Step 13

Finish pinafore. Try on pinafore and mark strap length for back. Sew to sash. Hem bottom edge with a narrow machine hem.

VARIATIONS

Use ¼″ check gingham as the material for a country pinafore and use the checks as a smocking guide.

Smock blouses, pillowcases and other items, allowing three times the finished width for the smocked areas when you are cutting the fabric.

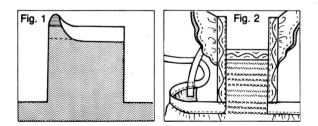

Fig. 1   Fig. 2

BATH RUG

Kathy hooked this Bath Rug in a jiffy with a speed hooking tool. The richly colored yarns of washable polyester form a rug that is both practical and decorative. The Bath Rug makes a different housewarming or shower gift and is wonderfully relaxing to work on.

MATERIALS

large pieces of paper, at least 3′ square

pencil

dressmaker's carbon

3′ square jute rug canvas[13]

wooden frame[1] 3′ square

stapler or small nails and hammer

speed hooking tool[13]

light-blue permanent marker

four 2½-oz. skeins of wheat-colored rug yarn[13]

seven to nine ½-oz. skeins of wine-colored tapestry yarn[13]

two ½-oz. skeins of tapestry yarn[13] in each of the following colors: yellow, bright green, dark blue, medium blue, pink

one ½-oz. skein of tapestry yarn[13] in each of the following colors: rust, light blue (or the above quantities of yarn in other colors of your choosing)

rug-backing latex[13]

ruler

edge-binding adhesive[13]

flat spatula

METHOD

Step 1

Using the instructions on page 150, enlarge the pattern on page 179 on paper and transfer to the rug canvas with dressmaker's carbon, marking each color section. Go over lines with permanent marker to make them easier to see. (See fig. 1.)

Step 2

Stretch the canvas on the frame, making sure that it is centered. There will be a 2½″ border around the pattern. Staple or nail one side, then tightly secure the opposite side. Repeat with the other two sides. It is important that the canvas be stretched as tightly as possible with the pattern centered and straight.

Step 3

Thread the hooking tool, follow the package directions for hooking, and outline each shape and then fill in. The loops should be of a medium-low height. (Lower loops are easier to clean and do not mat as easily as longer loops.)

Step 4

When the hooking is completed (and canvas is still in the frame) use a metal spatula to latex the back of the looped area, following the instructions on the latex can. The latex keeps the loops from coming out and makes the rug less likely to slide on the floor.

Step 5

Remove the rug from the frame when the latex has dried completely. Using a pencil and ruler, draw on the right side of the canvas a border 2½″ from the hooked rug edge. (See fig. 2.) Cut along the border line. Apply edge-binding adhesive to the back of border area. Let the adhesive dry until tacky, then turn the edge under 1″ and press firmly with fingers. At the corners, pinch border material together and miter. (See fig. 3.)

Step 6

Fold glued edge over to the back of the rug and with a pencil mark the place where the edge touches the back of the rug. (See fig. 4.) Spread adhesive glue over the back of the rug from the folded edge to the pencil line you have drawn and let the adhesive dry until tacky. Fold edge over to pencil line and press firmly with fingers. Pinch hem together at corners and cut along miters. Hand wash rug when necessary.

VARIATIONS

Hook pillow covers, place mats or seats for chairs.

Make a large rug by sewing smaller ones together. (Small rugs are much easier to work with than larger ones.)

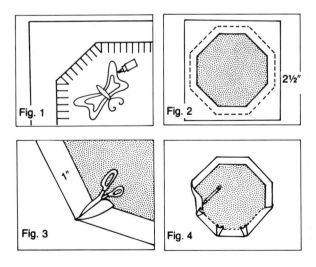

Fig. 1   Fig. 2   2½″

Fig. 3   Fig. 4

WATER LILY LINGERIE

Try your hand at this stenciling process and create a beautiful nightgown like the one pictured here. You'll sleep serenely when you wear your pretty Water-lily Lingerie.

MATERIALS

tracing paper and pencil

light-colored dressmaker's carbon

2 pieces of stiff paper about 8″ × 11″; shirt stuffers work well

X-acto knife and masking tape

1 small can or jar each textile paint [2] in white, yellow and medium-green

½″ stiff stencil brush

1 sea-green nightgown

medium artist's brush

clean cotton cloth

iron and ironing board

METHOD

Step 1

Using tracing paper, trace the water-lily pattern on this page and with your dressmaker's carbon transfer to stiff paper. Cut out with X-acto knife and lift out indicated sections, leaving a negative for your stencil. (See fig. 1.) One stencil is for the lily (white paint) and the other for the leaves (green).

Step 2

Decide where you want the leaves placed. Position the stencil for the leaf and tape in place. Add a little yellow to green paint to brighten the color, if necessary. Brush on the green paint evenly. Be careful not to smudge the leaf as you remove the stencil from the gown. Do all the leaves.

Step 3

After the leaves have been stenciled and the paint has dried, tape stencil for lilies on top of each leaf and paint with white. Let dry. With tip of artist's brush, make yellow dots in center of each lily for stamens.

Step 4

When leaves have been stenciled and the paint has dried completely, place a clean cotton cloth over the water lilies and press with a warm iron for several minutes on each side to help the paint set for maximum durability. Hand launder the nightgown.

VARIATIONS

Stencil a robe to match the nightgown.

Stencil water lilies on slips, petticoats and other underthings for lovely lingerie sets, using reduced versions of the patterns for smaller articles.

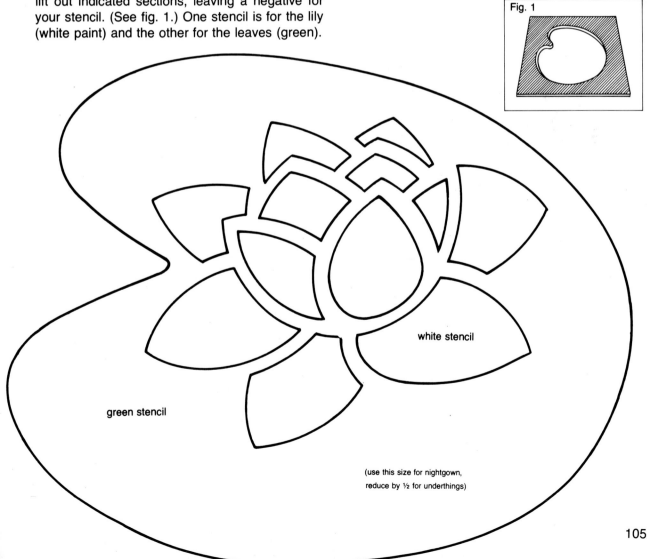

Fig. 1

white stencil

green stencil

(use this size for nightgown, reduce by ½ for underthings)

MOSAIC POT

Richie used the ancient art of mosaic to transform an ordinary clay flowerpot into a decorative planter. This project is just the thing for the plant lovers among you.

MATERIALS

12″ clay (preferable) or plastic flowerpot

pencil

1 yd. string

ruler

ceramic tile mastic[15]

approximately 200 ½″ square tiles[15] each in tan, light and dark peach (a total of 600 tiles)

tile nippers[15]

1 lb. tile grout (do not use acrylic grout)[15]

large bowl

spoon

water

2″ flat paintbrush

sponge

fine steel wool

silicone polish or liquid floor wax

METHOD

Step 1

Using the photograph as a guide, pencil the design on a clean pot, starting at the top and working down. (See fig. 1.) Work in sections. To divide the pot into equal sections, wrap a piece of string around the pot. Mark where the string meets itself and measure with ruler. Divide by four and mark section division on pot. (You will have to take about three of these measurements if your pot gets smaller toward the bottom.)

Step 2

Put some glue on the back of each tile and stick to the pot following the design and leaving a very slight space between tiles for grout as shown in fig. 2. (Be sure to keep the can of mastic tightly covered. Remove a small amount at a time, because it dries extremely fast.) If tiles need to be shaped or made smaller, cut with the tile nippers. Hold the tile between your thumb and fingers, place cutter blades on the tile and press.

Step 3

Mix grout and a small amount of water in a bowl until a thick, creamy paste is formed. Generously brush grout on the mosaic, completely covering the surface and filling in all spaces between the tiles.

Apply a generous amount of grout on the rim of the pot to cover the tile edges. Remove excess with a damp sponge and continue cleaning the surface until the grout is set. Clean bowl immediately after use.

Step 4

When completely dry, remove any remaining grout with fine steel wool. Wax with silicone polish or liquid wax.

VARIATIONS

Mosaic can be used on almost any surface. Cover a table top or the inside of a tray. Search for less than lovely objects in your home and beautify them.

Use small pieces of linoleum, wood, ceramic, marble or pebbles instead of tiles for your mosaic designs.

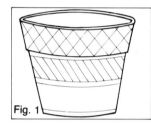
Fig. 1

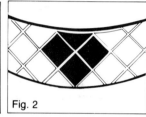
Fig. 2

APPLIQUE TOWELS

Transform ordinary terrycloth towels into decorator towels with country charm. This project is very easy. The patches are cut from scraps of coordinating fabric and are sewn to the towels by machine. You'll love the way these Appliqué Towels will add a fresh touch to your bathroom.

MATERIALS

tracing paper

pencil

carbon paper

stiff cardboard (shirt cardboards are fine)

mat knife

straight-edge ruler

⅛ yd. medium-checked red gingham, preshrunk and colorfast[10]

¼ yd. small-checked red gingham, preshrunk and colorfast[10]

⅛ yd. red cotton, preshrunk and colorfast[10]

tailor's chalk (optional)

clear plastic ruler

matching thread

pins

iron

a set of white terrycloth towels (as plain as possible)

sewing machine

METHOD

Step 1

Using tracing paper, trace the patterns on page 163 and with carbon paper transfer to cardboard. Using a straight-edge and mat knife, cut out cardboard patterns. Place patterns on wrong side of cotton and gingham fabrics and mark pattern edges with a pencil or with tailor's chalk. With a pencil and a clear ruler mark seam allowance ¼" in from all pattern edges. Carefully cut out on cutting lines.

Step 2

Using the photograph as a guide, place right sides together and stitch patches on penciled lines. Turn outside edges under on seam allowance and press.

Step 3

Pin completed patchwork piece on the widthwise center of the towel several inches from the bottom. (See photograph for placement.) Topstitch around edges of the patchwork piece.

Step 4

Cut a strip of material 2″ wide and the length of the towel width plus ½″ seam allowance. Turn all edges under ¼″ and press. Pin strip close to the edge of the towel and stitch. Towels often have a decorative flat space near the edge of the towel. Adjust the width of the strip to cover this space if necessary.

VARIATIONS

Sew a patchwork piece to the pocket of a terrycloth robe to give it a special look and make a tie belt in a coordinating fabric.

Make a set of hand towels with a seasonal motif. Sew a patch in the shape of a Christmas tree or angel on a green or red towel.

Make a set of hand towels for a lovely hostess gift.

RACING
WHEEL

Eric gave his car a custom touch with this Racing Wheel. The wheel is covered with leather and shellacked twine. It is easy to grip—your hands won't slip—and it doesn't get icy cold in the winter or red hot in summer. Make a Racing Wheel for your car. The process is easy, inexpensive, and the results are rich-looking.

MATERIALS

enough 4 to 6 oz. brown leather[5] to cover the spokes of steering wheel

sharp razor blade

contact cement

sharp knife

orange shellac

1″ flat paintbrush

⅛″-wide brown twine[16] (1 average-sized ball)

METHOD

Step 1

Cover the spokes of the steering wheel with leather. Cut a strip of leather that is equal to the length of the spoke plus enough leather to loop over the rim of the wheel (see fig. 1) and wide enough so that the leather will wrap about the spoke with about ½″ lap. With a razor blade, cut the part of the leather that goes over the rim of the wheel so that the leather is equal in width to that of the spoke plus ¼″ extra on each side. (See fig. 2.) Fold under the ¼″ allowance for a finished edge. Coat spoke, wrong side of leather and the part of wheel rim to be covered with leather with contact cement. Wrap leather around rim and around spoke so that the seam is on the underside of the spoke. Neatly trim off any excess leather with a sharp knife so that the seam edges are flush. (See fig. 3.) Cover the other spokes in the same manner.

Step 2

Using a paintbrush, coat the rim of the steering wheel with shellac. Let dry until sticky to the touch.

Step 3

Wrap the wheel. Start next to a spoke, holding the end of the twine against the wheel at a right angle to the wrapping direction, and wrap the ball of twine over the end. (See fig. 4.) Continue wrapping the twine around the wheel, leaving no spaces. When almost to the next spoke (with about ½″ more to wrap), make the final loops of twine loose, wrap to end, cut twine, leaving about ½″ extra, insert end under the final loops (see fig. 5) and pull tight. Trim the end of the twine as close to the loops as you can and push end under loops with point of knife.

Step 4

Finish the wheel by applying several coats of shellac, giving each coat plenty of time to dry in between applications. (One coat must be dry to the touch before applying the next.)

VARIATIONS

Wrap the handles of your bicycle. They'll look great!

Try wrapping furniture—arms of chairs, legs of tables, etc.

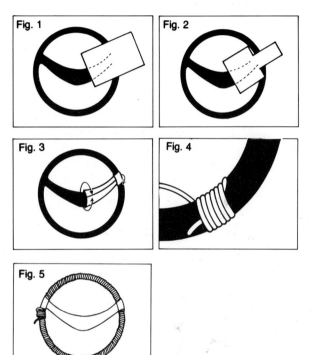

Fig. 1 Fig. 2 Fig. 3 Fig. 4 Fig. 5

SKINNY BELTS

Make two Skinny Belts to wear night and day. The passementrie belt, crocheted by Kathy, is made of silver elastic cord. The other is a go-with-everything natural-colored belt that Andrea braided and beaded. Both belts are made easily and at minimal cost.

MATERIALS

two 50-yd. spools of silver elastic cord[5] (Method I)

size C crochet hook (Method I)

sewing needle and thread (Method I)

one 1″ silver-colored horseshoe-shaped buckle[18] (Method I)

1 ball, approximately 150 yds., of ⅛″ natural-colored string[16] (Method II)

approximately 130 multicolored ¼″ beads[19] (Method II)

scissors (Method II)

METHOD I—The Silver Belt

Step 1
(See crochet instructions, stitches and abbreviations on page 152.) Make a crochet chain 33″ long or long enough to fit comfortably about the hips. (If you wish to make a waistline belt, adjust the length accordingly.)

Step 2
Crochet the belt. Row 1: sc in 2nd ch from hook and in each ch across row, ch 2, turn.
Row 2: (yo hook, draw up loop in first st) 3 times, yo and through all loops on hook for a cluster, ch 1 to close, * (yo, draw up a loop in next st) 4 times, yo and through all loops on hook, ch 1 to close (popcorn st made), repeat from * across, ch 2, turn.
Row 3: hdc to end of row, work 8 hdc in ch 2 from row 1, continue hdc along opposite side from popcorn sts, ch 1. Do not turn.
Row 4: sc around entire belt and fasten off.

Step 3
Weave ends of cord into belt. Attach cord to buckle and sc around buckle, stretching cord to give an even stitch. Fasten off.

Step 4
Make the belt loop. Ch 16. Row 1: sc across, ch 1, turn.
Row 2: repeat row 1.
Row 3: sc across, fasten off, sew ends of loop together.

Step 5
Finish the belt. Insert the prong of the buckle through the center of the belt one inch from the square end of the belt. Slipstitch edge to wrong side of belt to attach the buckle. Slip belt loop over the rounded end of belt and sew in place about 1¼″ from buckle (see photograph).

METHOD II—The String Belt

Step 1
Cut nine 100″ lengths of string.

Step 2
Place the nine lengths together with ends even. Take the ends of two of the pieces, wrap around the other pieces and knot about 9″ from one end of the string. (See fig. 1.)

Step 3
Braid the string, using three pieces of string for each of the three braid strands. Braid a 63″ length and knot as in step 2.

Step 4
About 4½″ from the knots that begin and end the braid, tie a small knot in each of the loose strands of string, slip on six to seven beads on each of nine strings at each end and knot again. Trim the string ends to ½″ from knot.

Fig. 1

MEXICAN
CANDLES

Light your dining table with these exquisite flowered candles. I first saw candles like the ones pictured here in Mexico and loved them. After a bit of experimenting I came up with the rather easy method below for transforming ordinary white candles into lovely floral ones. I think you'll enjoy working on this project and hope you will be as excited about the results as I am.

MATERIALS

double boiler

¼–½ lbs. of beeswax or several white candles[2] (do not use paraffin; it's too brittle)

1 package wax coloring[2] or 1 crayon in each of the following colors: dark green, red, rose, purple, dark turquoise, yellow

6 paper cups

baking sheet or wax paper

small knife and scissors

small artist's brush

tracing paper

pencil and paper

carbon paper

two 13″ white dripless candles

two candlesticks

2 scallop-edged cookie cutters[18], 1½″ and 2″ in diameter

METHOD

Step 1

Make the flowers one color at a time. In a double boiler melt about ⅙ of the wax for each color. (Beeswax makes the best flowers because it will mold without breaking.) Gradually add crayon shavings or bits of wax coloring until wax is the color you desire. Pour into a paper cup.

Step 2

For each flower, pour a small amount of wax onto a baking sheet or wax paper and let cool for a moment. With a cookie cutter cut a circle from the wax. (See fig. 1.) Cut two circles for each flower. Make 3″ circles for large flowers, 2″ circles for medium-sized flowers and 1½″ circles for small flowers. With fingers, mold one of the two wax circles for each flower into a cup shape. (See fig. 2.) Gently fold the other circle in half and then in half again. (See fig. 3.) The folded circle will form the center of the flower. With the brush, dab warm wax in the center of the cup shape and attach folded circle. For each candle make one large flower and two medium flowers in each of the following colors: green, red, rose, purple and turquoise. Make 18 small yellow flowers for each candle.

Step 3

Using tracing paper, trace the pattern for the leaves on page 165 and with carbon paper transfer to paper and cut out. Follow the instructions in step 1 and step 2 for the melting, coloring and pouring of the wax. Place the leaf pattern over the wax and trace around edge with knife to cut out. Warm the edges of the leaves with fingertips and curl under slightly. Make seven leaves for each candle.

Step 4

Place the white candles in candlesticks. For each candle join three leaves together at their bases (see fig. 4) and with a dab of warm wax attach to candles 5″ from their tops. With a bit of warm wax attach six small yellow flowers, edges touching, below the leaves. Directly beneath the yellow flowers attach one medium-sized flower in each color, then six small yellow flowers below the medium-sized and then five more medium-sized flowers below the yellow. You should now be about 8″ from the top of the candle.

Step 5

Attach four overlapping leaves 4″ from the bottom. Attach six small yellow flowers at the base of the leaves and directly below the yellow flowers attach the five large flowers. Now you're ready to plan a party!

VARIATIONS

Cover a large square candle with flowers.

Make one huge blossom, attach it to the top of a green candle and plant it in a flower pot filled with sand.

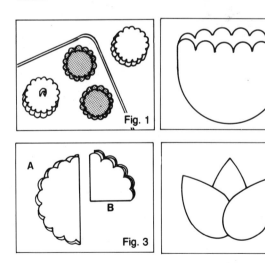

Fig. 1   Fig. 2   Fig. 3   Fig. 4

SCENT SATIONS

These Scentsations are lovely little bags filled with sweet-smelling scent or potpourri. Kathy made the ones shown here. Place them in the corners of your lingerie drawers, in your linen closet or in your travel bags. They are delightful as a bridal shower gift, a hostess gift or as a stocking stuffer.

MATERIALS

tracing paper (Methods I, IV, V, VI)

pencil (Methods I, IV, V, VI)

dressmaker's carbon (Methods I, IV, V, VI)

⅛ yd. muslin (Method I)

¼ yd. interfacing (Methods I, V, VI)

scissors (Methods I through VII)

small embroidery hoop (Method I)

1 skein embroidery thread each in magenta, variegated green, peach, coral, mauve, cream, pink, black, yellow (Methods I, II, IV, V, VI)

terrycloth bath towel (Methods I, II, VI)

iron and ironing board (Methods I, II, III, IV, VI)

¾ to 1 cup potpourri or scent [9] (Methods I through VII)

sewing machine (Methods I through VII)

light-colored permanent felt-tip marker (Method II)

4″ square petit-point canvas[1] (Method II)

3″ × 9″ piece of deep-pink velvet (Methods II, IV)

5″ × 8″ piece of pink calico with small piece of matching ribbon (⅓ yd.) (Method III)

pinking shears (Method III)

4″ × 8″ piece of pale-pink satin (Method V)

4″ × 8″ piece of pink gingham (Method VI)

7″ to 8″ piece of white eyelet edging (Method VI)

pins (Method VI)

4 skeins pink embroidery thread (Method VII)

1 skein green embroidery thread (Method VII)

#1 crochet hook (Method VII)

cotton saturated with scent (optional, Method VII)

METHOD I—Initial Pouch

Step 1

Select an initial you like from a book or an ad, trace with tracing paper and with dressmaker's carbon transfer to muslin. Place the muslin in an embroidery hoop, baste a square of interfacing to the back of the muslin and stitch the outline of the initial in split stitch, using two threads of magenta. (See embroidery glossary on page 153.) Use the variegated green thread to do the stems in stem stitch and the leaves in satin stitch. Do the flowers in satin stitch, using the photograph as a color guide. Fill in the initial with the satin stitch, using six strands of thread.

Step 2

Remove muslin from the hoop and place face down on a fluffy towel. Press with a warm iron. Trace a 4″ square around the initial (with initial centered) and cut out. Cut another 4″ square from the muslin for backing.

Step 3

With right sides of muslin squares together, stitch around edges, leaving a small opening. Trim edges to ¼″ from stitching, turn right side out, fill with scent or potpourri and slipstitch opening closed.

METHOD II—Heart with Dove

Step 1

Place canvas over the pattern on page 177 and trace pattern with light-colored permanent marker.

Step 2

Stitch the heart and dove with Continental stitch, using the pattern color key for the thread colors.

Step 3

When stitching is completed, dip canvas in warm water and stretch gently back to original shape. Place face down on towel and press with a warm iron. Cut out the heart shape.

Step 4

Use canvas as a pattern to cut out pink velvet for backing. With right sides together, stitch around edges of the heart, leaving a small opening. Trim edges. Turn right side out, fill with potpourri and slipstitch opening closed.

METHOD III—Calico Bag

Cut two 4″ × 4″ pieces of calico and stitch around three sides ½″ from edge. Press and trim edges. Pink unstitched edge. Turn right side out and fill with scent. Close bag by tying with a bow of matching ribbon. Tack bow to bag in two or three places.

METHOD IV—Velvet Strawberry

Step 1

Using tracing paper, trace pattern on page 177 and with dressmaker's carbon transfer to wrong side of velvet. Lightly mark embroidery lines on right side of velvet. (Make two.)

Step 2

Embroider leaves in green, using satin stitch and seeds in black French knots. (See embroidery glossary on page 153.)

Step 3

When stitching is completed, place velvet face up and steam, being sure not to touch the fabric with the iron. Smooth with fingers. Cut around strawberry shape, leaving a ½″ seam allowance.

Step 4

Place right sides together and stitch around edges, leaving an opening. Trim edges and turn right side out. Fill with scent and slipstitch opening closed.

METHOD V—Trapunto Butterfly

Step 1

Using tracing paper, trace pattern on page 177 and with dressmaker's carbon transfer to satin. Cut two butterfly shapes.

Step 2

Baste a piece of interfacing to one butterfly shape to support the embroidery.

Step 3

Stitch on all lines with a machine straight stitch or an embroidery outline stitch, using six strands of matching thread. (See embroidery glossary on page 153.)

Step 4

When stitching is completed, place right sides of butterflies together and stitch around the edges, leaving an opening. Trim edges, turn right side out, fill with scent and slipstitch opening closed.

METHOD VI—Daisy

Step 1

Using tracing paper, trace pattern on page 177 and with dressmaker's carbon transfer to gingham. Cut two daisy shapes. Baste a piece of interfacing to the gingham piece you will embroider.

Step 2

Follow the indicated colors in the pattern and embroider with a satin stitch. (See embroidery glossary on page 153.) When stitching is completed, place embroidery face down on a towel and press.

Step 3

Shirr the eyelet edging carefully and pin around the outside edge of the calico circle. Attach eyelet to the calico with tiny running stitches.

Step 4

With right sides together, stitch around the edge of calico, leaving an opening. Trim edges, press, turn and fill with scent. Slipstitch opening closed.

METHOD VII—Crochet Rose

Step 1

See crochet instructions, stitches and abbreviations on page 152. Use a double thickness of embroidery thread throughout. Make the rose with the pink thread. Ch 4, sl to join, forming a ring.

Row 1: ch 1, work 11 sc in ring, sl to join.

Row 2: sc in first st, *(2 dc in next st, sc in next st), repeat from * 4 times. Do not turn after any row.

Row 3: sc in center back of first petal (in sc of first row), *(ch 3, sc in center back of next petal), repeat from * 4 times, sl to join.

Row 4: *(sc, ch1, 3 dc, sc in loop), repeat from * in each loop, sl to join.

Row 5: *(sc in center back of next petal, ch 4), repeat from * 4 times, sl to join.

Row 6: *(sc, ch 1, 2 dc, 1 tr, 2 dc, sc), repeat from * in each loop, sl to join.

Row 7: *(sc in center back of next petal, ch 4), repeat from * 4 times, sl to join.

Row 8: *(sc, ch 1, 3 dc, 1 tr, 3 dc, sc), repeat from * in each loop, sl to join, fasten off.

Step 2

Use double thickness of thread throughout. Make leaf with green thread. (Make two.) Ch 8.

Row 1: sc in second ch from hook, and in each ch, ch 2. Do not turn.

Row 2: 2 dc in next sc, 1 dc in next sc, 1 hdc in next st, 1 sc in each of next 3 sc, 5 sc in next sc (tip of leaf), sc in each of next 3 sc, hdc in next sc, dc in next sc, 2 dc in next sc, sl to join, leaving a three-inch thread.

Step 3

Use double thickness of thread throughout and make sachet pouch with pink. Ch 4, sl to join, forming a ring.

Row 1: ch 1, work 8 sc in ring, sl to join.

Row 2: ch 1, *(sc in next st, inc in next st), repeat from * around row, sl to join.

Row 3: ch 1, *(sc in next 2 sc, inc in next st), repeat from * around row, sl to join.

Row 4: ch 1, *(sc in each of next 3 sc, inc in next st), repeat from * around row, sl to join.

Row 5: ch 1, *(sc in each of next 4 sc, inc in next st), repeat from * around row, sl to join.

Row 6: ch 1, *(sc in each of next 5 sc, inc in next st), repeat from * around row, sl to join.

Rows 7 through 9: ch 1, work sc in each sc around row.

Row 10: ch 1, *(sc in each of next 5 sc, dec in next st), repeat from * around row, sl to join.

Row 11: ch 1, *(sc in each of next 4 sc, dec in next sc), repeat from * around row, sl to join.

Row 12: ch 1, *(sc in each of next 3 sc, dec in next st), repeat from * around row, sl to join, fasten off.

Step 4

Assemble the crocheted rose. Sew the two leaves to the underside of the rose on opposite edges. Stuff pouch with potpourri or cotton saturated with scent. Sew last row of pouch to row 7 of rose. Fasten off and weave in ends.

VARIATIONS

Create designs of your own and fill with scent.

Fill a tiny basket with crochet roses for an unusual gift.

Fill your Scentsations with home-made potpourri, giving them the ultimate personal touch.

CAKE
DECORATE

A beautifully decorated cake can be the highlight of a party. The luscious one shown here would be perfect for a Welcome to Spring celebration or for any festive occasion. Try your hand at cake decorating using the simple method below and you'll soon find yourself turning out cake masterpieces.

MATERIALS

two 10" round cake layers, each 2" high

4 cups white confectioners' frosting (can, package or favorite recipe)

metal spatula

1 recipe icing for flowers (below)

6 small mixing bowls

spoon

food color paste[7] in red, yellow, blue

#127, 104, 67, 14, 7, 3, 1 decorating tips[7]

pastry tube[7]

#6 flower nail[7]

wax paper

ICING RECIPE

4 cups sifted confectioners' sugar

²⁄₃ cup butter or margarine or ¹⁄₃ cup butter or margarine and ¹⁄₃ cup solid white vegetable shortening

1 teaspoon vanilla

2–4 tablespoons milk or cream

Cream shortening, add vanilla and gradually mix in the sugar. Add milk or cream gradually, stopping when mixture is fairly stiff.

METHOD

Step 1

Frost cake with metal spatula. Be sure that you invert the top layer (i.e., bottom side up) so that the top of the cake is level. Smooth the frosting and let set while making the flowers.

Step 2

Tint the icing for the flowers, using a very small amount of coloring to achieve delicate, pastel shades. Separate the icing into six bowls and add blue for the blue flowers, yellow for the yellow flowers, a bit of red for the pink flowers, a mixture of red and blue for the violet flowers and a mixture of yellow and blue for the green leaves.

Step 3

Prepare to make the flowers. Fill a pastry tube ¾ full or less with icing. Cut out as many 2" squares of wax paper as the number of flowers you are making. Attach one of these squares to the top of the flower nail with a bit of icing.

Step 4

Make the flowers. Hold the flower nail between thumb and forefinger of one hand and slowly turn counterclockwise while the other hand holds the pastry tube at a 45° angle to the top of the nail and controls the flow of icing as the nail is being turned. (See fig. 1.) Make all the flowers of one color at the same time. Be sure to wash pastry tube thoroughly before filling with a new color. Follow the instructions below for the individual flowers.

Step 5

Jonquil: Use tip #104 with the wide end touching the center of the nail and the narrow end just above the surface of the nail. Turn the nail while squeezing the yellow icing from tube and bring the tube out toward the edge of the nail and back toward the center to shape the first petal. The curved or cupped shape of the petal (see fig. 2) is achieved by moving the tip with a slight upward motion as you complete the petal. Make six petals, pinching the petal tips slightly for an authentic look. Make the center of the jonquil with #3 tip and top center with little yellow dots. Carefully slide wax paper off nail and set flower aside to dry.

Step 6

Wildrose: Make the pink petals of the wildrose with #104 tip, using the method described in step 5, but make the petals a bit shorter and closer together and do not pinch. (See fig. 3.) Use #1 tip to make the yellow stamens for the center of the flower. Remove from nail and let dry.

Step 7

Violet: Using tip #104, place wide end touching center of nail, narrow end turned slightly out. As you slowly turn the nail, move the tube filled with violet icing out toward edge of nail about ½" and then back to form petal. Make two more petals like this and two half their size. (See fig. 4.) With #1 tip make two yellow stamens in the center of flower. Remove from nail and let dry.

Step 8

Bachelor Buttons: Using tip #7 and blue icing, make a circular base (see fig. 5). Using tip #1, make several pointed lumps of blue icing to form flower center. With #14 tip make several small blue petals around the center while turning nail. Continue making rings of these petals until base is completely covered. Remove flower from nail and set aside to dry.

Step 9

Daisy: Place a bit of white icing in the center of flower nail. Place both ends of #127 tip on the outer edge of flower nail and move tube toward the center dot to form the first petal. (See fig. 6.) Continue making petals (they should touch each other about halfway down) until a flower is formed. Using tip #1, make a yellow center in the flower and flatten it a bit with a moisten fingertip.

Step 10

Rose: Using tip #127, build a 1″ cone-shaped mound of pink icing. Hold the tip perpendicular to the nail. Start with a firm pressure and relax the pressure as the cone builds. Now make the center bud. Hold the tube at a 45° angle with the wide end of tip touching the mound about halfway up and the narrow end slightly out, in a vertical position. (See fig. 7). While turning nail, squeeze out icing, swinging tube up from starting point, around top of mound and then down to starting point (see fig. 8). Now make a row of three petals. Place wide end of tip on mound about halfway up with the narrow end of the tip pointed up (see fig. 9). Turn nail and move tip up and down in an arc shape, increasing pressure on the tube on the upward swing, decreasing pressure as you swing down. Repeat this motion two more times to form the other petals. Using the same technique, but turning the narrow end of the tip out a bit more, make a row of five petals just below the row of three, with the second placed so that the petals fill in the spaces of the first row. (See fig. 12.) Make one more row, near bottom, of seven petals, using the same method as above but with the narrow end of the tip turned out even farther. Slide finished rose off nail and set aside to dry.

Step 11

Using #67 tip, squeeze green icing out on wax paper in a leaf shape. When leaf is the size you want, pull tip up and out to form point. Set aside to dry.

Step 12

When all flowers and leaves have dried and hardened a bit, arrange on cake and secure with a dab of frosting.

VARIATIONS

Decorate cupcakes with one large flower on each individual cake.

Decorate a ring cake.

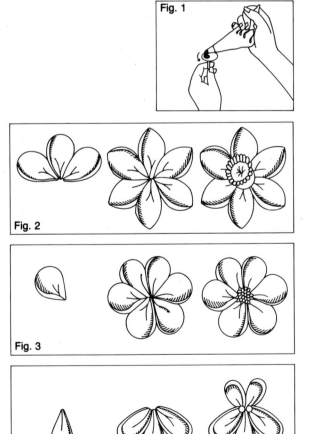

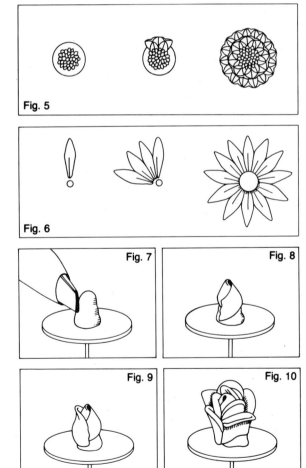

PIPE CHAIR

This ultra-modern chair has all the good looks and comfort of an expensive piece of furniture, but not the price tag. It's a bargain! The chair is rugged and easy to assemble. The frame is constructed of plastic pipe, bought in precut lengths, and the seat and back are made of canvas. My furniture-making experience is quite limited, yet I found this project a cinch!

MATERIALS

13 pieces of PVC pipe[16] 1¼″ in diameter (measured from outer edge to opposite outer edge), 7 pieces 28″ long; 6 pieces 23″ long (#1, 3, 10, 11, 12, 12)

6 side outlet elbow rail fittings[16]

6 single sliding socket tees[16]

4 pieces of 90° elbow rail fittings[16]

masking tape

1 pt. white high-gloss enamel or 1 can of spray white high-gloss enamel

1″ paintbrush (optional)

1 can polyvinyl chloride cement[16]

1 can polyvinyl chloride solvent[16]

scissors

iron and ironing board

pins

1 yd. of 45″-wide canvas (in any color that complements your decor)

sewing machine

heavy thread in color that matches canvas

METHOD

Step 1

Cover 1″ of both ends of each pipe with masking tape. Using regular or spray paint, paint uncovered parts of each pipe, the rail fittings and socket tees. If spray paint is used, use only out of doors or in a workshop, since it tends to drift over a wide area.

Step 2

After paint is completely dried, remove masking tape and clean ends of pipe thoroughly with solvent. Use solvent in a well-ventilated area only.

Step 3

Refer to fig. 1 for the assembly of the chair frame. Starting at the bottom of the chair, fit pipes 1, 2, 3 and 4 into four of the side outlet rail fittings. (See fig. 2.) Cement each pipe into fitting as you assemble.

Step 4

Fit pipes 5, 6, 7 and 8 into the top openings of the rail fittings (see fig. 3).

Step 5

Fit single sockets on the ends of pipe 9 (see fig. 4) and slide sockets down pipes 6 and 7 until 9 is about ten inches from the ground. Fit single sockets at both ends of pipes 10 and 11. Slide sockets on pipe 10 down pipes 5 and 6 and sockets on pipe 11 down pipes 7 and 8 until pipes 10 and 11 are even with each other and about 15½″ from the ground. Do *not* cement in position.

Step 6

Prepare the canvas seat and back. Cut a 21″ × 45″ piece of canvas for the seat and a 11″ × 45″ piece for the back. Fold the 21″ sides and the 11″ sides under ¼″ and press. Fold the same edges over ¼″ again and topstitch.

Step 7

Take the canvas seat bottom and stretch the 45″ length across from pipe 10 to pipe 11. Fold edges of canvas over the pipes, allowing some ease, and pin close to pipe. Machine stitch along line marked by pins. Trim ends of canvas to within ½″ of stitching line, fold ends under ¼″ and press. Fold under ¼″ again and stitch through both thicknesses of the canvas, forming a tube on each side to go over the pipes. Remove pipes 10 and 11 and slide ends of canvas seats onto pipe. Reposition pipes and glue in place. (See fig. 5.)

Step 8

Measure, hem and stitch back as you did seat in step 7. Slide the canvas back on pipes 6 and 7. Attach pipe 12 to the tops of pipes 5 and 6 with 90° elbow rail fittings. Attach pipe 13 to pipes 7 and 8 in the same fashion.

VARIATIONS

Paint the pipes and fittings with contrasting colors or cover them with fabric or shellacked twine (see Racing Wheel, page 110).

Make a cube shape from the pipes and fittings, have glass cut to fit the top of the cube, and you have a coffee or end table.

Make a child's chair from sections of broom handles and regular pipe fittings.

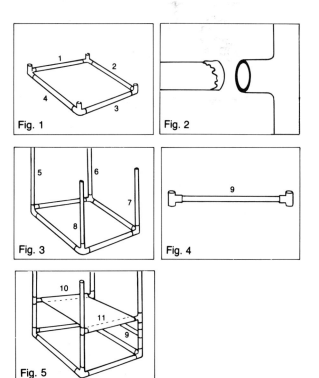

Fig. 1

Fig. 2

Fig. 3

Fig. 4

Fig. 5

WOODEN BRACELETS

These beautiful laminated bracelets are one of my favorite projects. Wooden bangles are the perfect accessory for today's natural-fiber clothes. The different tones in various kinds of wood provide the contrasting laminations. As you can see from the photograph, I experimented with many different laminations, using symmetrical and random patterns, arranging wood from dark to light tones. I used dark walnut, rich, ruddy Philippine mahogany, medium-tone maple and cherry and warm, light birch and oak. Gary made these bracelets with power tools, and I suggest that you try working with them too. They are, of course, much faster than hand tools. The square bracelet is the easiest to make, the circle and octagonal ones more difficult.

MATERIALS

two or more pieces of different kinds of wood[4] 4″ × 4″ in ⅛″, ¼″ and ½″ thicknesses

one piece of wood[4] 4″ × 8″ (of any of the three thicknesses above) for the handle

several pieces of open coat coarse, medium and fine sandpaper

piece of cotton or soft, clean cloth

compass[17]

white glue

cardboard

pencil

two 4″ C clamps[21]

carbon paper

hand or electric drill with ¼″ bit[21]

hand or electric jigsaw with several blades for cutting wood[21]

1′ broomstick handle or dowel of like diameter

very fine steel wool

fabric garden gloves

small block of wood for sanding block

small bottle of linseed oil[21]

METHOD

Step 1

Stack the wood in the order you want to create your bracelet design. Try mixing the colors of the woods as well as the thicknesses of the laminations. The 4″ × 8″ piece of wood should be placed at one end of the stack. It will serve as a handle to make your sawing easier, and the extra 4″ can be cut off and used later. (See fig. 1.)

Step 2

Sand all rough edges and clean all surfaces with cotton or cloth, leaving *no* dust. Spread a small amount of white glue on all surfaces to be bonded. Put a square of cardboard at each end of the glued stack to protect surfaces, clamp tightly with two C clamps, let glue dry overnight and remove clamps. (See fig. 2.)

Step 3

With the aid of the compass, trace one of the patterns on page 172 to cardboard, cut out, center pattern on wood and mark interior circles on wood with pencil. Note: There are two lines for the wrist hole on each pattern ⅛″ apart, a cutting line and a sanding line. Make two patterns for each bracelet design, one for the sanding line and one for the cutting line.

Step 4

Drill a hole in the exact center of the bracelet large enough for the blade of the saw to pass through. Use this as a guide to mark the bracelet pattern on the other side of the wood. Fasten one end of the blade in the saw, slip free end of blade through hole and fasten in the other end of the saw. (See fig. 3.) Saw with even up-and-down strokes (perpendicular to wood surface), following the cutting line top and bottom. (When finished you should have a 2⅜″ rough-cut opening.) Remove saw blade.

Step 5

Wrap the coarsest sandpaper around broomstick handle or dowel and sand inside bracelet with circular motion. Repeat with medium and fine sandpapers and finish with fine steel wool. (Garden gloves will protect your hands.) The opening should now measure 2½″ and should be sanded to its final finish.

Step 6

Line up the centers of the pattern and the bracelet exactly and trace outside line onto wood with a pencil. Saw along line with even up-and-down strokes.

Step 7

Sand first with coarse sandpaper, then with medium and fine and finish with very fine steel wool. If you make a square or an octagonal bracelet, use a sanding block (a piece of sandpaper wrapped around a piece of wood with a true flat surface). Bevel the corners if you wish.

Step 8

Bring out the full beauty of the wood by rubbing it with a small amount of linseed oil. Gary and I enjoy this part of the project because it is so exciting to see the dramatic change the linseed oil produces in the wood.

VARIATIONS

After practicing with the patterns I've given you, try some shapes of your own.

Use the leftover pieces of wood to make buttons, rings and cufflinks. Remember that squares, rectangles, etc., are easier to make than circles and ovals.

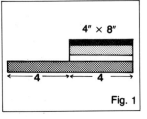

Fig. 1

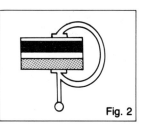

Fig. 2

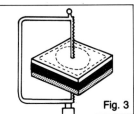

Fig. 3

CACTUS COAT RACK

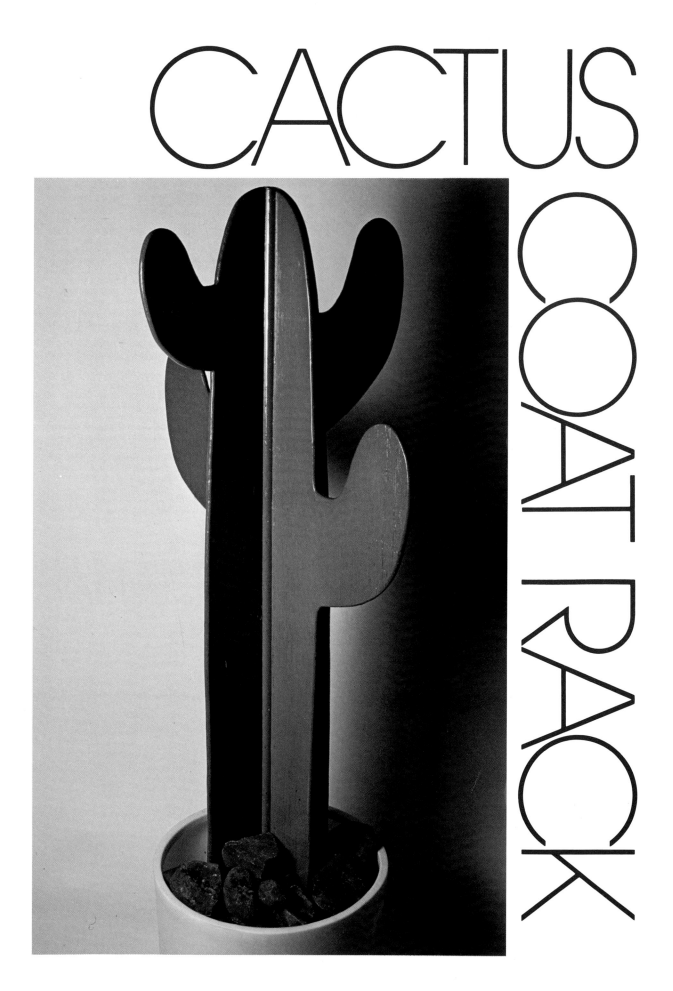

Here is an unusual coat rack for your entrance hall, bedroom or children's room. The Cactus Coat Rack is practical, colorful and guaranteed not to be prickly.

MATERIALS

a large piece of paper at least 4' × 8'; you may use newspaper pages taped together

pencil

several sheets of carbon paper

two pieces of ½" interior-grade plywood at least 4' × 8'; examine the wood for imperfections; the quality of plywood varies greatly

electric saber or keyhole saw or hand saw[16]

flat wood rasp[16]

several sheets of fine, open-coat aluminum oxide or garnet sandpaper

white glue

four 96" pieces of ¾" quarter-round corner molding

1 box #4 finishing nails

hammer

1 pt. green gloss latex paint

1 pt. clear wood sealer

2½" flat paintbrush

clean, lintfree cloth

100-lb. bag all-purpose cement

large tub and broom handle to mix cement

15" to 18", or larger, round flower pot

sand or rocks to cover cement in flower pot

METHOD

Step 1
Using the instructions on page 150, enlarge the pattern on page 178 to full size on paper. With pencil and carbon paper trace pattern to plywood.

Step 2
Cut out pattern shape from plywood pieces with saw. Saw one of the two shapes in half lengthwise. (See fig. 1.)

Step 3
File all outer edges with a wood rasp.

Step 4
Sand the surface of the cactus pieces with fine sandpaper, using straight strokes in the direction of the grain.

Step 5
Place the whole plywood shape on a flat surface. Apply white glue to the straight edge of one of the half-shapes and center it on the whole shape. (See fig. 2.) Glue the edges of two of the 96" molding strips and place them on either side of the glued half-shape, flush against the sides of the shape. (See fig. 3.) Nail the molding in place with finishing nails and, if necessary, with the saw trim the top and bottom of the molding so that they are flush with the cactus edges.

Step 6
Turn the cactus on the other side and support it with four chairs (see fig. 4.) so that you can attach the remaining half-shape, following the instructions in step 5.

Step 7
Brush on one coat of the clear wood sealer over cactus. When the sealer is dry, brush on a coat of green paint. Let dry. Sand lightly with fine sandpaper, dust the surface thoroughly and apply another coat of paint.

Step 8
Mix the cement according to the package directions. (The quantity of cement you will need will depend on the size pot you are using.) Fill the pot about one third full with cement, set cactus in the pot and pour the remaining cement into the pot to within about three inches of the top of the pot. Let the cement harden and then sprinkle sand or rocks over the cement to cover.

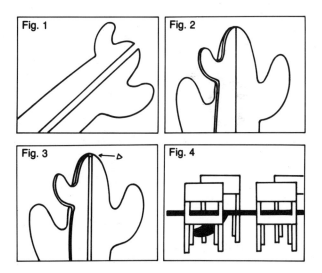

Fig. 1 Fig. 2 Fig. 3 Fig. 4

DRIED FLOWERS

Flowers lend a warm, decorative touch to any room. This project lets you have pretty bouquets all year round at a minimum of cost. Dry your summer favorites and arrange them in a pretty vase, container or basket. Drying flowers was once a long, tedious process, but with the simplified method below you'll find it a quick and easy hobby that achieves lovely results. (See note at end of project for lists of flowers that dry well and those that do not.)

MATERIALS

flowers at the peak of their bloom and with no moisture on their petals or leaves, flower buds or autumn leaves

knife

1 to 2 lbs. silica gel[2] (despite its name, silica gel is in powdered form)

large coffee can (or one of similar size) or cookie tin with lid

masking tape

artist's brush

floral wire[19]

florist's tape[19]

florist's clay[19]

florist's foam[19]

clear acrylic spray[19]

METHOD

Step 1

Cut off flowers, leaving 2″ stem below flower blossom.

Step 2

Pour about 1½″ silica gel into the can. Place flowers face up and buds and foliage in a horizontal position in the gel. (The flowers, buds or foliage should not touch each other.) Gently pour silica gel slowly over the flowers, etc., covering each petal. You must do this carefully in order to maintain the natural shape. Cover completely with gel.

Step 3

Cover the can with lid and seal with masking tape. Put the can in a place where it will remain undisturbed for a few days. Small flowers like daisies will take about two days, larger ones up to seven days. You'll have to do some testing. The flowers will wilt if they have retained any moisture and will break if overdried. They should not feel too soft or too brittle. Don't hesitate to put them back into the gel if you think they need it.

Step 4

Remove the flowers by slowly pouring off gel until the flowers are uncovered and then gently lift them out. Brush the rest off with a soft artist's brush. I recommend that the flowers be stored in a dark

place in an airtight container with a little silica gel in the bottom until you are ready to make an arrangement. Silica gel may be used over and over again as long as the blue crystals do not turn pink. If the crystals turn color, bake at 250° in a large uncovered pan for 30 minutes or until crystals are back to the blue color.

Step 5

Make stems for your dried blossoms. Place a piece of florist's wire next to the 2″ stem and wrap around stem and wire with florist's tape. Continue to wrap down wire until you have the desired stem length. Cut the wire and the tape. Remember that the flowers are fragile. If a petal should fall off, glue it back with a bit of white glue. To preserve your flowers, spray them lightly with acrylic spray three times, waiting 15 minutes between each application.

Step 6

Fill in your dried flowers with baby's-breath, cattail weeds or strawflowers. These can be dried by hanging bunches upside down in a dark area for seven to fourteen days. Spray dried cattails with hair spray or acrylic spray after they have dried to preserve them.

Step 7

Arrange your bouquet when the weather is dry. Put the flowers in a vase as I did or anchor a piece of florist's foam with florist's clay in the container you are going to use. Insert the wire stems into the foam one at a time. Arrange from the center out, using the tallest flowers or filler in the center. Try to balance not only the height of the flowers but also the colors. Let the flowers and leaves hang over the edge of the container. You can also make a vertical arrangement (to put under a glass dome, for example). Center a florist's frog on the bottom of your container and put a long rectangular piece of florist's foam (vertically) onto the spikes. Then arrange flowers and filler. Remember, this arrangement will be seen from all sides.

NOTE

FLOWERS AND FOLIAGE THAT DRY WELL:	
asters	lilies-of-the-valley
autumn leaves	marigolds
baby's-breath	orchids
camellias	pansies
carnations	peonies
chrysanthemums	poppy foliage
cornflowers	roses
daisies	sage
dogwood	snapdragons
forget-me-nots	zinnias
gardenias	
gladioli	FLOWERS THAT DO NOT DRY WELL:
heather	
hyacinths	anemones
hydrangea	azaleas
lavender	daffodils
lilacs	lilies
	tulips
	violets

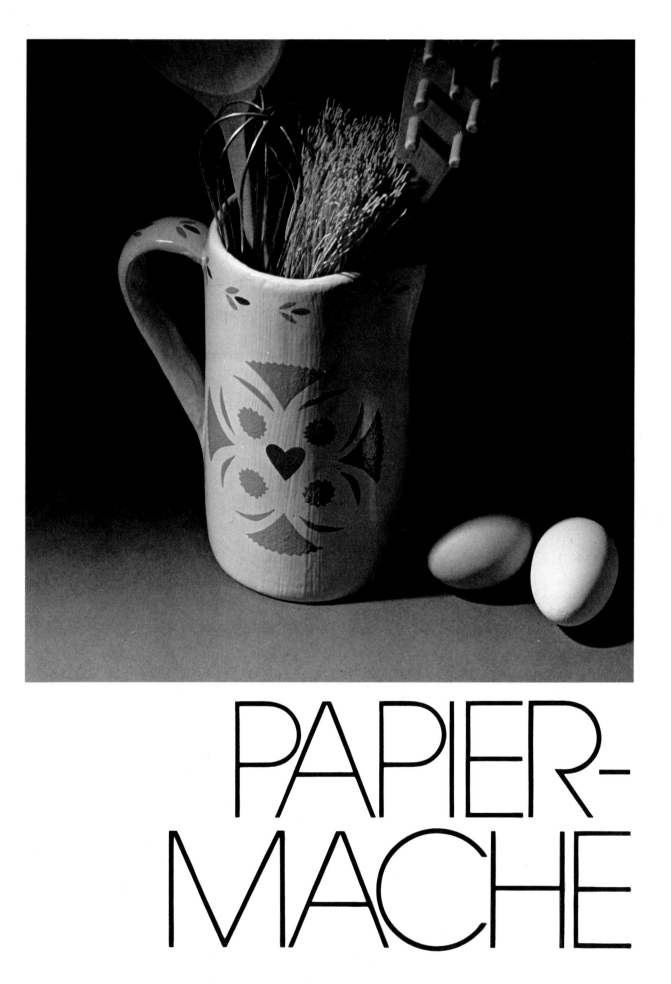

PAPIER-MACHE

Make this Papier-Mâché Pitcher with American folk art stencil design. Its homey naiveté makes it a perfect accessory for country-style kitchens. Use it to store wooden spoons and other small utensils. This project is very inexpensive and one of the easiest in the book.

MATERIALS

several sheets of newspaper

several sheets of color comic pages from newspaper or comic book

several sheets of paper toweling

metal-edged ruler

scissors

empty cylindrical oatmeat box without top

8″ × 10″ piece of cardboard; a shirt stuffer will do nicely

masking tape

tracing paper

pencil

carbon paper

white glue

bowl

sponge

1″ paintbrush

white gesso[2]

1 sheet fine sandpaper

X-acto knife

1 small jar each tempera paint[2] in green, white, red, brown

stencil brush

clear acrylic spray or clear shellac and brush

METHOD

Step 1

Tear paper in 1″ strips by ripping against the edge of a ruler, making three groups—one of newspaper, one of comic pages, one of paper toweling. Set aside.

Step 2

With pencil and ruler, draw four equally spaced lengthwise lines from the top of the oatmeal box to ½″ from the bottom. Mark a dot at the bottom of each line. At the top of the box mark off ¼″ from each side of each line. Draw a line from the ¼″ mark on either side of each line down to the dot to form narrow triangles (see fig. 1). Cut out these triangles

with scissors, bring cut edges together (but not overlapping) and tape with masking tape (see fig. 2). This procedure tapers the box and gives it a pitcherlike shape.

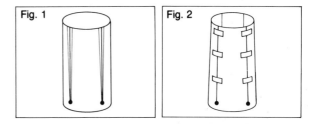

Step 3

Using tracing paper, trace the pattern for the spout on next page and with carbon paper transfer to cardboard. Cut out. Fold cardboard on fold lines and tape spout to box so that the upper edges of spout are even with the edge of the box. (See fig. 3.) Cut out cardboard that blocks spout.

Step 4

Cut a ⅝″ × 7″ piece of cardboard. On the side of the box directly opposite the spout, tape cardboard strip about 1½″ from the top of the box so that the length of the strip extends up from the taping. (See fig. 4.) Bend the strip down to form a handle and tape the other end.

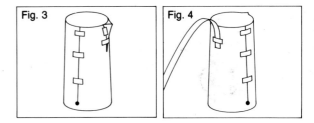

Step 5

In a bowl, mix about ½ cup of white glue with ½ cup of water. With sponge, brush or fingers, apply glue to both sides of the strips of paper toweling and cover the entire pitcher—body, handle and spout with the glued strips. Press the strips firmly to the pitcher, smooth out wrinkles and wipe off excess glue with sponge. Be sure to continue applying the strips over the lip and into the pitcher for about 5″. The strips should overlap each other slightly. Apply the comic-paper strips next in the same manner and then apply the newspaper strips. Apply each layer of strips in a direction opposite to that of the former layer for added strength.

Step 6

Set pitcher on a flat surface to dry. Drying will take about two days. If not completely dry after that time, keep pitcher in a warm oven with the door ajar until it is dried.

Step 7

Paint entire surface of pitcher, inside and out, with white gesso and let dry. Sand lightly with fine sandpaper. Add additional coats for more shaping if desired.

Step 8

Using tracing paper, trace the stencil design on this page and with carbon paper transfer to cardboard. Cut out with X-acto knife.

Step 9

Mix a bit of brown tempera into some white and paint the inside and outside of pitcher with the resulting cream-colored paint. Let dry.

Step 10

Add a bit of white and a bit of brown to the green tempera for a pale-green color. With one hand hold the stencil in place and, using a stencil brush, paint the sections to be colored green. Let dry.

Step 11

Mix a bit of white and a bit of green into the red tempera for a muted red. Paint the sections of the stencil to be colored red, following the method described above. Let dry.

Step 12

Spray pitcher with clear acrylic or brush on clear shellac. Let dry and fill with wooden spoons and other utensils.

VARIATIONS

Papier-mâché is tremendously versatile. Use it to make pencil cups, small toys, jewelry, masks, tree ornaments, etc.

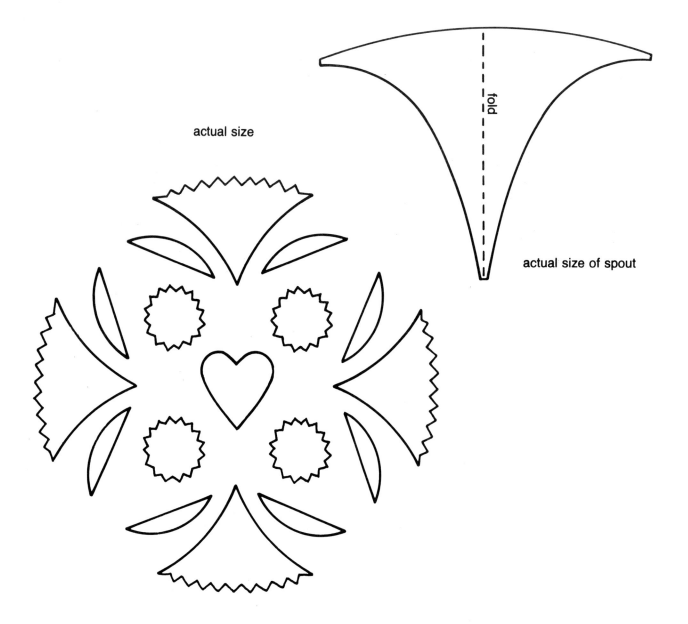

actual size

fold

actual size of spout

PILLOW
WEAVE

Weaving is a fascinating process and a simple, satisfying and expressive hobby. The following project for a yarn and leather pillow is an easy and inexpensive way to try your hand at this old art. The pillow may be made entirely from your stock of leftover knitting, crocheting or needlepoint yarn and scraps of leather or you may wish to start fresh with new supplies. Needlepoint yarn usually may be bought in small amounts, and it is very colorful. If you don't have leather scraps, you can buy leather in small quantities from many craft supply houses.

MATERIALS

a wooden frame for loom at least 15″ square[2,16]

hammer

small box of nails

yarn, leftover, or small skein in each of 4 or 5 colors you choose

ruler

large, blunt needle

wide-tooth comb or large fork with wide-spaced tines

scissors

8–15 strips of leather[5] (several different widths and the length of the pillow plus 2″)

fabric for pillow back

pencil

loose pillow stuffing (such as foam, kapok, polyester, old nylon stockings)[10]

sewing machine (optional)

4″ x 5″ card

METHOD
Step 1
Make your loom. Looms can be made of anything from the wooden stretcher of an old painting (canvas removed) to a wooden picture frame, four pieces of wood nailed together or a section of an outdoor wooden chaise longue. Hammer a row of nails ½″ apart down each of two parallel sides of the frame you have selected. You now have a two-harness loom ready for weaving. (See fig. 1.) Should you prefer a closer weave, use more nails, placed closer together and staggered. (See fig. 2.)

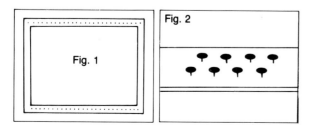

Step 2
Pick a color scheme. For best results use no more than four or five colors on your first project. I used related colors, but you might try all earth tones, pastels, primary colors or just plain white. A single color can be beautifully effective if you mix various fibers such as wool, cotton and silk with different leathers such as suede and kidskin.

Step 3
String loom. The most basic terms in weaving are "warp" and "filling." The warp runs vertically the length of the weaving and the filling runs across the warp. The warp is the base of your weaving and should always be strung with the strongest material. In this project the filling is the leather strips and yarn. To string the warp, take a several-yard length of your strongest yarn in the color you want to run up and down. Hold the loom in your lap or place on a table top. Form a slip knot at one end of the yarn (see fig. 3), loop the slip knot around the lower outside nail and pull until firm. Using even tension, string the yarn back and forth across the loom until you have the desired width of your pillow plus 2″. (See fig. 4.) You are now ready to weave.

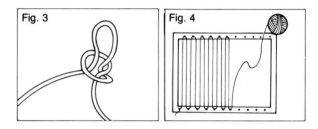

Step 4
Thread the longest blunt needle you can find (needlepoint needles are perfect) with about six pillow widths of yarn of a color other than the one of your warp. Guide the needle under and over the warp threads. Pull the yarn, leaving an extra inch at the side. Repeat the procedure in the other direction and be sure to go over the warp thread you went under the last time. (The pattern you create with this method is called tabby or plain weave.) Do five rows to start, then, later, as many as you like.

Step 5
Use a large comb or fork to beat or press the yarn uniformly together each time you add a row. Continually check to see that your weaving is even.

Step 6
Cut the leather into strips ⅜″, ¾″ and 1¼″ wide and as long as the width of the pillow plus 2″. The leather is woven like the yarn except that you use your fingers as a guide rather than a needle. It is woven only once. Experiment with yarn and leather placement, using the photograph as a guide. Try blending several colors together or use many strands of one color.

Step 7

When you have woven the pillow to the desired size, do five or six rows of plain tabby. Carefully slip your work off the nails and run two rows of machine stitches at each end to prevent unraveling. (A survey once reported that more homes have sewing machines than bathtubs. If you happen to have a bathtub but no sewing machine, do the stitches by hand.)

Step 8

Choose a fabric for the pillow back. Felt is easy to use and very colorful, as are some wool fabrics. Leather is very elegant if a bit expensive. Pin right sides of weaving and backing together. Mark guidelines for stitching. (See fig. 5.) Stitch, leaving a 3″ side opening. Press and trim edges to ½″. Turn right side out. Stuff, doing corners first, and slipstitch opening closed.

Step 9

To make tassels, wrap yarn around a 4″ x 5″ card about ten times. Slip a piece of yarn around the strands, tie securely (this is the top of the tassel) and remove the card. Wrap another piece of yarn around the yarn bundle near the top, knot and let the ends fall in place. (See fig. 6.) Sew on tassels and clip them in proportion to the pillow.

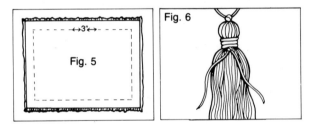

Fig. 5

Fig. 6

VARIATIONS

Now that you have mastered the basic weaving techniques you are ready to experiment. Make some colorful place mats, a wall hanging or make several woven squares to be sewn together for a skirt or a simple wrap jacket. Just use your imagination—and have fun!

SEWING BASKET

Pictured here is a Sewing Basket with the timeless beauty of wood marquetry. New techniques, materials and tools have made the art of marquetry much easier and less time-consuming than it was in the past. How nice it is to be able to organize sewing equipment in a box that is pretty enough to display!

MATERIALS

pencil

tracing paper

7″ wide wooden octagonal box² (the one pictured here has 4″ and 2″ alternating sides)

1 combination package of wood veneers[4] (eight kinds and colors)

dressmaker's carbon

cellophane tape

veneer saw or very sharp X-acto knife[4]

1 small can veneer glue[4]

veneer roller[4]

1 small can benzine[16]

clean cloth

1 small can plastic wood[16]

1 sheet each of coarse, medium and fine aluminum oxide sandpaper

1 small container white shellac[16] (optional)

1 small container alcohol[16] (optional)

1 small can boiled linseed oil (optional)

handsome brass hinge and fastener[16]

fine steel wool

paste wax

METHOD

Step 1

Trace the top and sides of your box onto paper. (See fig. 1.) Use the pattern on page 173 for your design or create a simple, geometric design of your own. Select the veneers you wish to use, arranging them in contrasting shades of wood.

Step 2

When you have decided on your design and veneer arrangement trace the design on paper and code the design for the placement of the various types and colors of veneer. (See fig. 2.) Place a piece of dressmaker's carbon face down on the top of the box. Transfer the design with code to the box by taping the paper face up on the box over the carbon paper and then tracing over the lines of the design with a pencil. Remove design and tracing paper from the box and transfer the design with the dressmaker's carbon to the appropriate pieces of veneer. This entire step must be done as accurately as possible.

Step 3

Using an X-acto knife or veneer saw, cut out veneer pieces carefully and place the cut pieces on the traced design to be sure they fit.

Step 4

Brush glue over the entire top of the box, following the instructions on the glue can. Start at the corner or edge and begin placing veneer pieces. Brush the wrong side of each piece with glue and press firmly in place on top of box. Follow the design carefully, fitting pieces together. Always work with adjacent pieces, progressing across the top. (See fig. 3.) Roll each piece with the veneer roller and remove excess glue with a cloth moistened with benzine.

Step 5

Do the sides of the box in the same manner, filling in any crevices with plastic wood. After glue and plastic wood have dried, sand the entire surface, starting with the roughest sandpaper and working down to the finest. Sand in the direction of the grain or in a circular motion. Remove the sawdust with a cloth moistened with benzine.

Step 6

Attach the hinge to the cover and box and the fastener to the opposite side of the box and cover. (See fig. 4.)

Step 7

Mix equal parts of alcohol and white shellac and brush a coat of the mixture onto the box. (The shellac becomes clear when mixed with the alcohol.) Let dry thoroughly. Rub the surface with steel wool. Apply two more coats. Mix another batch of shellac and alcohol, using 75% shellac and 25% alcohol, and apply two coats of this mixture. (Be sure to allow one coat to dry completely before applying the next and sand with steel wool after each coat except the last.) Or, if you wish to take a short cut, rub box with a clean cloth and a small amount of boiled linseed oil.

Step 8

Wax with a paste wax and you are finished.

VARIATIONS

Line the box with felt. Trace on paper the inside of the box bottom and use as a pattern to cut felt. Measure the depth and circumference of the box and use these dimensions to cut a strip of felt for the sides. Glue pieces in place with white glue.

Cover a table top with marquetry or decorate a plain frame using marquetry.

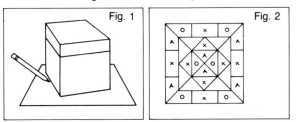

Fig. 1   Fig. 2

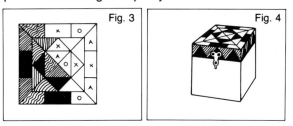

Fig. 3   Fig. 4

MONO GRAMS

Initial almost anything to make it distinctively yours, or put a friend's initials on a gift for a truly personal touch. Although most initialing is done by a silk-screen process, this project uses another, much more simple method that makes personalizing a snap.

MATERIALS

Mystic tape

wax paper

press-on letters[2]

X-acto knife

small piece of cardboard

textile ink[2] (Speedball, for example)

medium-size brush

small piece of fabric; cotton would be best

iron

METHOD

Step 1

Roll out on wax paper a strip of tape wide enough for initial. You may have to use two or three strips side by side, but avoid piecing an initial itself.

Step 2

Transfer press-on letters to tape and smooth. Cut around letters carefully with X-acto knife and lift out. The "negative" that remains is your stencil.

Step 3

Remove wax paper from the stencil. Position stencil on the surface of the article to be initialed and press down firmly. When stenciling things such as T-shirts, put a piece of cardboard under the area being stenciled to prevent the ink from seeping through to other areas.

Step 4

Brush ink on smoothly, let dry 15 minutes and remove the stencil. (The stencil may be reused if it is still sticky.) Wash the brush immediately with water.

Step 5

Place a clean piece of fabric on top of the letters and press with a medium-warm iron for three to five minutes to set the ink for maximum washability and durability. Repeat on the wrong side of the letters.

VARIATIONS

Monogram fabric suitcases, tote bags, golf bags.

Use silk-screen paint and monogram glass and lucite items.

ID BRACELETS

There is a special satisfaction and excitement involved in working with a precious metal. The following project gives you the opportunity to experience these feelings as you create beautiful contemporary ID bracelets from sterling silver. My brother Gary, a fine craftsman, made these bracelets with professional results. This project requires a lot of patience if you have never worked in silver before, for you must go slowly and very carefully to produce the best results. Don't be frightened by the list of tools. Most aren't expensive and some can probably be borrowed.

MATERIALS

black felt-tip marker

a piece of 16-gauge sterling silver, 1″ × 5⅜″ (available at hobby shops)[4]

½″ Roman letters in stencil pattern from dime store

compass

hand or electric drill with smallest bit[21]

jeweler's saw with medium or deep well plus a dozen #2 blades[3]

vise[16]

1 half-round tapered jeweler's file[3]

1 square-tapered jeweler's file[3]

several pieces each of coarse, medium, fine and very fine close coat sandpaper

masking tape

2′ length of heavy conduit pipe with 2″ diameter[21]

small block of wood for sanding block

leather, rubber or wooden mallet[3]

steel wool

fabric garden gloves

METHOD

Step 1

With a black felt-tip marker cover with ink the side of the silver that is to be the outside of the bracelet (this is called bluing).

Step 2

Select the initials you want in the bracelet, center them and trace very carefully to the silver with the pointed end of a compass.

Step 3

Drill a hole, large enough for the saw blade to pass through, in each section of the letters to be cut out. (See fig. 1.)

Step 4

Insert top end of the saw blade, with teeth facing handle, into top of saw and slip free end of blade through one of the drilled holes into bottom of saw.

The blade must be taut, so press top and bottom of saw together and secure end of blade. Saw to one of the letter lines and follow the line. It is rather easy to snap a blade, so don't become alarmed if you do so. It is easier to saw when the silver is held in a vise, but you can do without one if necessary.

Step 5

After you have cut out the letters, true up the edges and corners with the jeweler's files. Use the square file for corners, the round one for curves. Always hold the file perpendicular to the silver and file with up-and-down strokes.

Step 6

Wrap four layers of masking tape around the pipe and clamp in a vise. With the leather, wooden or rubber mallet shape the bracelet around the pipe, starting in the very center of the bracelet. (See fig. 2.) This is the most difficult part of the project and must be done carefully and slowly. Don't try to pound the bracelet into a crude shape to be refined later; you'll never get the bumps out. Try on bracelet and correct shape if necessary.

Step 7

You are now ready to sand. Wrap the coarsest sandpaper around a piece of wood that has a flat surface (you may staple the paper on if you wish). Sand with long, even strokes down the length of the silver until all the black has been sanded off and there are no pits or low spots. Sand edges, corners and backs. Then sand with medium sandpaper in the same way, then with fine and very fine.

Step 8

Rub the bracelet with steel wool in lengthwise strokes to produce a satin finish. (Garden gloves will protect your hands.) For the really shiny finish shown in the photograph, take the bracelet to a jeweler for buffing or buff it yourself if you have access to a buffing wheel. Keep your bracelet in top shape by cleaning occasionally with silver polish.

VARIATIONS

Try simple designs such as a heart, star or zodiac sign instead of initials.

Make a pendant by cutting out one initial on a square of silver, drilling a hole in the top, inserting a small ring and hanging the pendant from a black leather cord.

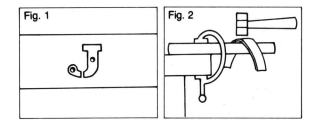

Fig. 1

Fig. 2

FRIENDSHIP QUILT

This Friendship Quilt is just what the name implies; it is made of self-portraits created by friends and relatives. My friends made squares that were completely different, ranging from appliqué, embroidery and batik to three-dimensional stuffed figures, macramé and permanent-marker sketches. It's great fun collecting the squares, for they are often surprisingly unique.

MATERIALS

48 patches made by your friends

scraps of material for fill-in patches (if needed)

scissors

4 yds. of 45″ wide brown cotton fabric for backing, joining strips and border

1 package rolled quilt filling[17]

pins

brown thread

needle

sewing machine

iron and ironing board

30′ of $5/16$″ brown grosgrain ribbon

METHOD

Step 1

Write your friends and ask them to make patches for your project. The self-portrait should be done in appliqué, patchwork, embroidery or any other medium they choose and should be signed in embroidery or with permanent marker. The idea is that the square be a description of its maker, a literal or symbolic portrait. The patches don't have to be perfect or professional-looking. Some of my favorites were the more primitive patches. Each patch should be 6″ square plus a ½″ undecorated seam allowance on all sides of preshrunk cotton or similar fabric.

Step 2

Make the backing for the quilt. Cut the backing fabric in two 2-yd. lengths and, using a sewing machine, join the pieces with a lengthwise seam (right sides together). Press seam. This seam will go down the center of the width of the backing. The backing should be cut to a piece that measures 63″ × 48″. Mark this size area off with pins on the fabric (keeping the seam centered) and cut around the perimeter of the backing. Do not cut into the excess material; you will need 60″ strips that must be cut from the excess material.

Step 3

From the material that remains after the backing has been cut out, cut: five 2½″ × 60″ strips and forty-two 2½″ × 7″ strips for the joining, two 3½″ × 60″ strips and two 3½″ × 48″ strips for the border.

Step 4

When you have received all the patches, work them into a pleasing visual arrangement. Fill in, if necessary, with extra patches, embroidered with a heart, for example. Divide patches into six rows of eight patches each. Stack each row into a pile and number each patch and row.

Step 5

Join the patches together. Work row by row, sewing the first patch in a row to a 2½″ × 7″ strip on the ½″ seam allowance. (See fig. 1.) Join the next patch to the strip and the opposite side of the patch to another strip. Work across until all but the outside edges of the first and last patches in a row are joined horizontally to a strip. Join the patches in the remaining rows in a similar fashion.

Step 6

Join the rows. Sew each row to a 2½″ × 60″ strip on the ½″ seam allowance.

Step 7

Sew lengthwise borders to patchwork edges on the ½″ seam allowance. Then sew on the widthwise borders.

Step 8

Place backing face up and patchwork face down over it. Roll out quilt filling over patchwork and trim to same size as patchwork and backing. Baste the three together on the ½″ seam allowance, leaving an opening of about 14″ for turning. Machine sew around the edge, trim corners to ⅛″ and turn right side out. Slipstitch opening closed.

Step 9

Cut the ribbon on the diagonal in 4″ strips. Sew the ribbon to the quilt. Stitch through the ribbon and the quilt about two times and knot thread on ribbon. Tie ribbon in a knot to cover stitches. (See fig. 2.) Sew the ribbon along the border first. Place ribbon in line with the centers of the joining strips (see photograph). Be sure that the filling is smooth and evenly distributed before sewing. After the border ribbons have been attached, work from the center of the quilt and sew a ribbon where each joining strip intersects another. Be sure to smooth the filling as you sew.

VARIATIONS

Use the quilt as a wall hanging.

Make a coverlet instead of a quilt by omitting the stuffing.

Change the theme of your quilt. Make a flower quilt or one with miniature landscapes.

Make a child's quilt with a number, alphabet or animal theme.

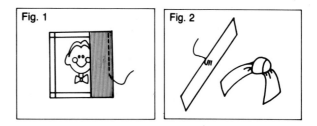

Fig. 1   Fig. 2

BOOK
BINDING

Leather has elegance, simplicity and natural appeal. It is easy to work with; all you need are a few simple tools. The book shown here has inside pages made of fine rice paper that is sewn in the book through holes punched in the leather. These books make great appointment calendars and look handsome on a home or office desk.

MATERIALS

a 9½″ × 15½″ 6 to 8 oz. piece of cowhide[5] (have it cut to size in the shop where you buy it)

#2 or #3 edge beveler[5]

a V gouge[5]

pencil

awl or ice pick

heavy-duty needle with large eye

approximately 16 to 32 sheets of 20″ × 30″ rice paper[2] (rice paper varies greatly in weight; buy more of the light-weight, less of the heavy-weight)

triangle

leather cream

sharp mat knife

1 spool white carpet thread

several felt-tip permanent markers in various colors (I used rust, tan, orange, wine, turquoise, peach, yellow

METHOD

Step 1

Place the leather flat out, right side up on a drawing board or kitchen cutting board. Place the V-shaped notch of the bevel tip at a 45-degree angle against the edge of the leather and push forward to cut a thin sliver off the edge. This rounds the edges of the leather, giving them an attractive appearance and preventing them from curling up or fraying. Bevel all the edges. (See fig. 1.)

Step 2

Place the leather face down and mark gouging lines for spine with pencil as indicated in fig. 2. Place V gouger on the start of one line and push forward lightly. Do the same on the other line. (This is done on thick leather to make it fold easily.) If the leather doesn't fold easily on line, score again.

Step 3

Mark holes on the spine with pencil as shown in fig. 3. Use the thonging chisel and hammer or an awl to punch the holes on right side of leather.

Step 4

With pencil, mark squares and border using the photograph as a guide.

Step 5

Use the photograph as a guide and draw on the leather with the permanent markers. Polish the book cover with leather cream, following the package directions.

Step 6

Prepare the pages. Cut the rice paper into 9″ × 14″ pieces, using a triangle and marking cutting lines with pin pricks. (See fig. 4.) Line up the ruler with pin marks and cut with a mat knife. Match edge of paper and fold in half. Place pages inside one another, forming 16-page bundles called signatures. Make enough signatures to fill a ½″ space when stacked.

Step 7

Thread the needle with carpet thread and stitch signatures through holes as shown in fig. 5. Color outside thread with a permanent marker.

VARIATIONS

Make a small book for addresses or memos or an oversized one for a family album.

Make a small book, fill it with your favorite recipes and give it as a bridal shower gift.

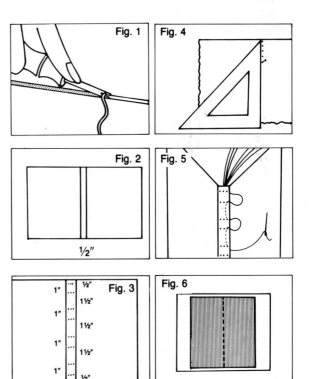

VALENTINE

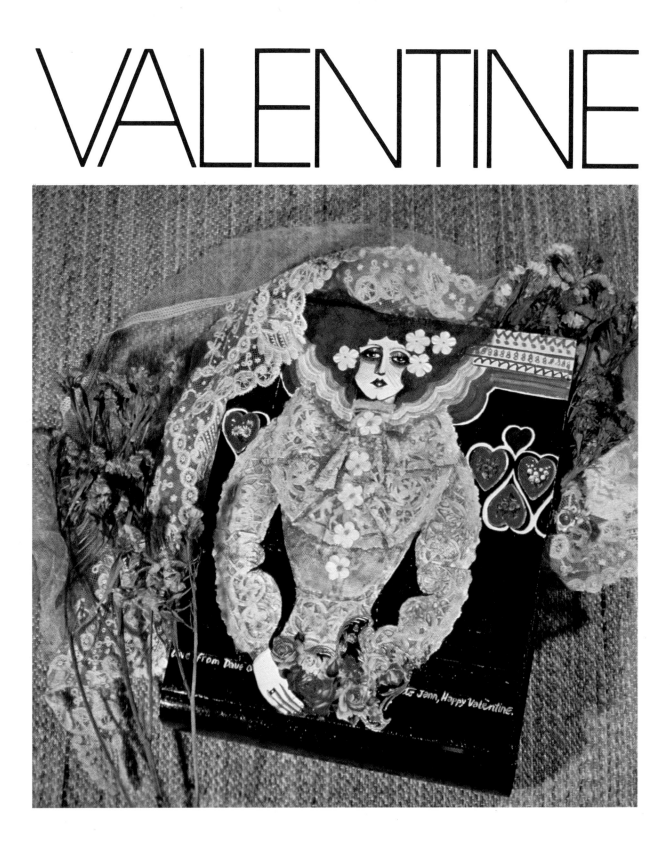

Surprise your valentine by sending that special person a unique remembrance like the one David made, shown here. Send it filled with home-made sweets. When the box is empty, it becomes the perfect place to store small treasures.

MATERIALS

tracing paper

pencil

light-colored dressmaker's carbon

wooden cigar box

small can of white gesso[2]

flat ½" paintbrush

fine artist's brush for painting details

1 small tube acrylic paint each of navy, medium blue, red, burnt sienna, white, violet (or substitute colors you like)

2 paper doilies

white glue

5 or 6 small red paper hearts[3]

9 to 12 small white fabric flowers[17]

clear acrylic spray

METHOD

Step 1

Paint a clean cigar box with white gesso and let dry.

Step 2

Trace the pattern on this page for the basic figure and details and transfer to dry cigar box with light-colored dressmaker's carbon.

Step 3

Paint the background of the box navy. David painted the hands and face white, the hair red, eyes blue, clouds violet and outlines for the hearts white. Duplicate this color scheme or paint with other colors you like. Add other decorations or paint a message if you wish. Let dry.

Step 4

Cut doilies out in the shape of the dress, folding small tucks at the collar to give a three-dimensional effect. Hold in place on box with plenty of white glue. Let dry and then paint with a very light mixture of white and burnt sienna paint to give a sepia finish.

Step 5

Glue on the hearts and flowers and use a generous amount of glue to attach the small white flowers down the front of the dress and in the hair. Use the photograph for a guide. Let glue dry and spray with clear acrylic spray. Fill box with home-made candy or cookies for a valentine sure to be remembered.

VARIATIONS

Change the theme of the box. Make a birthday box filled with candy and small toys for a child, or a memory box for a grandparent filled with the grandchildren's artwork, photographs, etc.

enlarge twice (see page 150)

TREE TRIMMERS

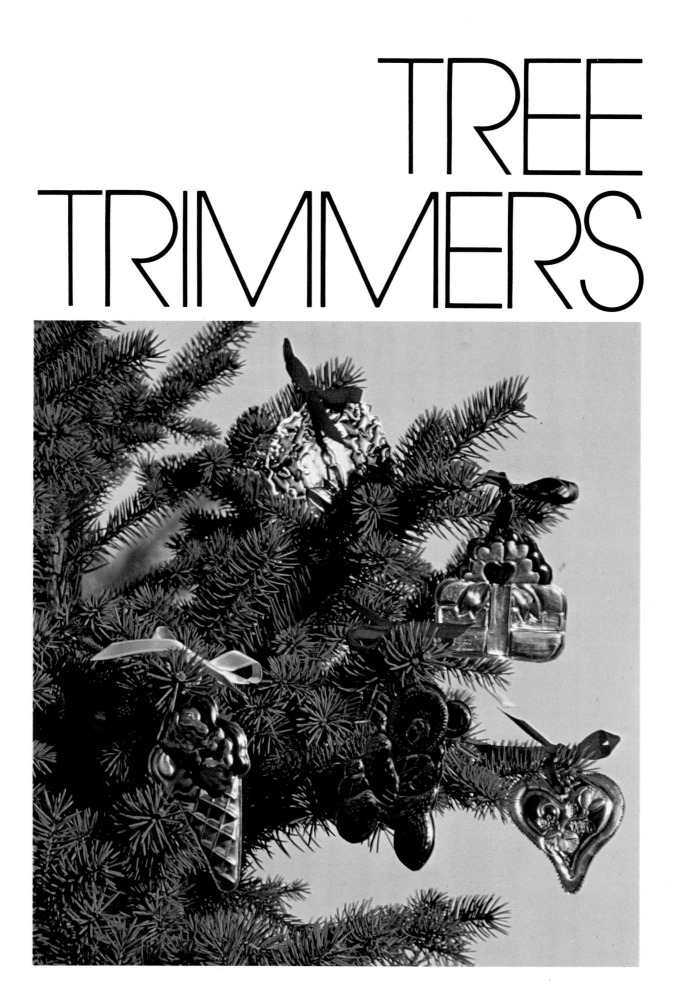

These shiny ornaments, hung with ribbons, will brighten your Christmas tree and will give it a personal touch. The Tree Trimmers are made of hand-embossed aluminum foil and are painted with bright colors. Start early so that you can make many in time for Christmas.

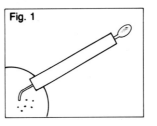

Fig. 1

MATERIALS

tracing paper

pencil

1 foot of #36 (.005) aluminum foil[2] (for six ornaments) 10"–12" wide

heavy-duty scissors or shears[16]

wooden styling tool with one pointed end, one rounded end[2]

nail or icepick

1 jar each translucent paint[2], such as Glass Stain, in rose, blue, yellow, green, purple, red

small artist's brush

a total of about 2 yds. of ¼"-wide satin ribbon in several colors which coordinate with the paint

METHOD

Step 1

Using tracing paper, trace patterns on page 180 Place tracing paper over dull side of aluminum and retrace all the lines with pencil. These lines will be impressed on the metal.

Step 2

Cut out shapes with scissors. Punch a hole with a nail or icepick where indicated for hanging. Note that all corners should be rounded. (Be careful not to cut yourself on the edges.)

Step 3

Use photograph and patterns as guides for surface decorations, raised lines and details. Draw the smaller of these with the pointed end of the styling tool on the wrong (dull) side of the aluminum. Use the smoother, rounded end of the tool for the larger details. (See fig. 1.)

Step 4

Using the photograph as a guide, paint the pieces, using the paintbrush and undiluted paint on the shiny side of the metal. Let dry, string with ribbon cut to desired length and hang on tree.

VARIATIONS

Make a greeting card out of the aluminum or print a favorite poem for framing. (Remember to write all words backward on the wrong side of the metal.)

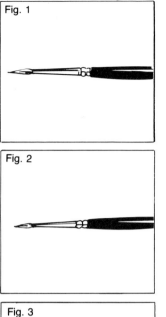

Fig. 1

Fig. 2

Fig. 3

Fig. 4

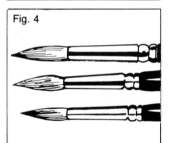

Fig. 5

Fig. 6

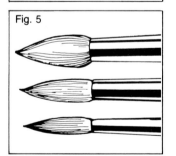

MATERIALS

As you will note, each project is headed by a list of specific materials needed to complete that project. These materials are the ones I used, but in many cases, other materials can be substituted with good results. Use your own judgment in making such substitutions. Unusual items in each listing are followed by a number. These numbers correspond to those in the Sources for Materials section on page 155, which gives the general sources as well as the names, addresses and telephone numbers of stores where these materials may be purchased.

Below are descriptions of some of the basic materials needed for the projects:

X-acto knife. An X-acto knife cuts a clean, sharp, straight edge. You can buy this knife in the art-supply store. Blade #11 is a good all-purpose blade.

Mat knife. This is a sturdier version of the X-acto and is used to cut heavier items. Mat knives can be purchased at art-supply stores.

Brushes. I recommend buying good-quality brushes. If you take care of them, they will last much longer than less expensive ones and will not leave hairs in your work as cheap brushes will. Test a brush for resilience by pushing the hairs of the brush back. When released, the hairs should spring back to their original position. Never, never leave a brush standing in paint, water, turpentine, etc.

The three kinds of brushes you will need most often are:

Artist's or watercolor brushes. Used in projects requiring brushes other than paint or stencil. Artist's brushes can be purchased at art-supply stores. Below is a list of brush sizes and the work for which they are used:

0–1 (fig. 1) for very fine work
2–4 (fig. 2) for fine work
5–7 (fig. 3) for medium-sized areas
8–10 (fig. 4) for medium to large areas
10–18 (fig. 5) for large areas such as backgrounds
Numbers 2, 6 and 10 will probably serve all your needs.

Paintbrushes. Flat brushes for applying paint, glue, etc., to large surfaces. I recommend that you have ½", 1" and 2" brushes on hand. Hardware stores carry a wide range of good-quality paintbrushes.

Stencil brushes (see fig. 6). These brushes come in a range of sizes like the artist's brushes, but a # 2 or 3 is all that you'll need. You'll find stencil brushes in art-supply stores or hobby shops.

ENLARGING AND REDUCING

The easiest way to enlarge or reduce a pattern is to have it photostated to the desired enlarged or reduced size. Most photostat shops will do this for you gladly at a charge that varies according to the size of the photostat, but which is usually quite low. If you want to change the size of a pattern yourself, use the following procedure. Using tracing paper, trace the pattern and transfer to paper with carbon paper. Using a clear plastic ruler and a pencil, mark a grid of

squares over the pattern and label each square across the top with numbers and each square down the right side with letters. (See fig. 7.) I use ¼" squares for small designs and ½" to 1" squares for larger designs. Now on a second sheet of paper mark off another grid with the same number of squares but of a size that represents the number of times the pattern is to be enlarged or reduced. For example, if your original grid was composed of ½" squares and the pattern is to be reduced by half, the second grid would be made up of ¼" squares. If the design were to be enlarged to twice the original size, the second grid would be made up of 1" squares. Label the second grid exactly as you did the first. Copy the design from the first grid to the second, working square by square, making sure that the design is kept in proportion.

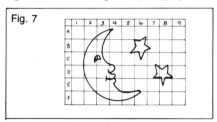

Fig. 7

NEEDLEPOINT GLOSSARY

The Continental Stitch. This stitch (see fig. 8) is made working from right to left. Bring the needle from the back of canvas through a hole on the right side of your work to the front and insert needle through the hole that is one row above and diagonally to the right of the hole you started from. Bring needle from back through the hole to the left of the starting point and repeat stitch until the row is finished. Turn the canvas completely around so that the stitched row is now on the bottom and begin next row. The Continental is an uncomplicated stitch—very good for the beginner. It makes the best straight lines and is very good for details. Its one disadvantage: It tends to warp the canvas with a strong diagonal pull. Blocking will rectify this warp.

The Basketweave Stitch. This stitch (see fig. 9) is begun with two Continental stitches. The third stitch is made by bringing the thread up through the hole (a) directly under the beginning hole and inserting the needle in hole (b), making a stitch that covers the threads intersecting directly under the first stitch. Make stitch four by bringing the needle out through hole (c) directly under the hole (a) that was the starting point for stitch three. Insert needle in hole (d) to make a stitch that will cover the threads that intersect directly under stitch three. Stitch five is formed by bringing thread out of hole (e) that is directly left of the bottom of the third stitch and inserting needle in hole (f) directly to the left of the top of stitch three. Form two more Continental stitches next to the ones already made and continue the diagonal stitching procedure as above. If you try the stitch on a piece of canvas you will see that it is far less complicated than it appears to be, though it would be advisable for beginners to use the Continental on their first project. The great advantage of this stitch is that it doesn't warp the canvas as much as the Continental. The basketweave stitch is particularly good for large areas of background because the canvas is not turned every row as it is with the Continental.

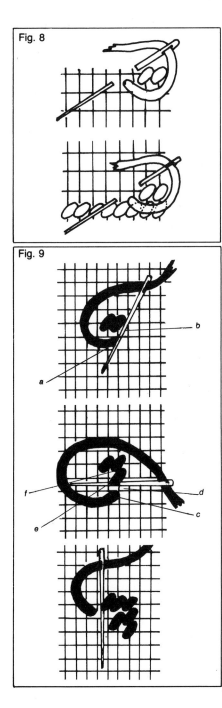

Fig. 8

Fig. 9

BLOCKING NEEDLEPOINT

Professional blocking gives needlepoint a finishing touch that is hard to duplicate at home. However, the instructions below will help you block with good results. Cover a drawing board, or some other flat surface in which you can stick pins, with brown paper and secure paper with rustproof tacks or staples. Draw the original outline of your needlework (using pattern or canvas measurements) on the paper. Use a ruler and a triangle to true up any straight lines or corners of the outline. With a clean, wet sponge, moisten the needlepoint until quite wet (but not dripping). Place the needlepoint canvas face down in the outline you have drawn, stretch canvas to the corners of the outline and tack. Start with center of one side and stretch and tack along edges on out-

line. Next do the opposite side. Stretch and tack the third and fourth sides. The fourth side can be rather difficult to stretch into shape. Don't be afraid to tug and pull; needlepoint is amazingly strong. Let the stretched canvas dry for two or three days. Remove tacks. The needlepoint surface should look smooth and even since it has been on its face during the blocking. Fluff up the surface a bit, if you wish, with the steam of a steam iron held over, but not touching, the needlepoint. Blocking may have to be repeated to achieve really good results.

HOW TO STITCH AND STUFF A SIMPLE PILLOW

First, choose a fabric for the pillow back. The backing fabric should be of a weight similar to that of the front. Using the front as a pattern, cut the backing to size. With a ruler and tailor's chalk, mark seam lines on the wrong side of the backing. Pin back and front with right sides together and stitch on seam line, leaving a 3" side opening. (Leave a wider opening for large-size pillows.) Press, trim edges to ½" and turn right side out. Stuff pillow with kapok, polyester fiber fill or cotton, or with a foam-pillow form. I don't recommend foam chips; they tend to make a pillow lumpy. It's a nice touch to insert a small muslin bag filled with potpourri or scent with the stuffing. After the pillow has been stuffed, slipstitch opening closed.

KNITTING GLOSSARY

Casting on. Make a slip knot on needle, leaving about a two-yard tail of yarn. Hold yarn tail in palm of left hand and needle with slip knot in right hand. Loop end of yarn around left thumb (see fig. 10) and wind yarn coming from ball loosely around right-hand fingers. Insert needle into loop around thumb from front to back and pass yarn in right hand over needle from back to front. Draw yarn through loop on thumb, slip loop off thumb and pull to tighten. Your first stitch is cast on. Repeat the above until you have on needle the number of stitches required by pattern.

Knit Stitch. With needle holding the cast-on stitches in the left hand, slip point of right needle into front of first stitch from below as shown in fig. 11. (The yarn is guided by the right hand and held to the back of work.) Pass yarn under, then over right needle, pull yarn forward through stitch and slip original stitch off left needle. You now have one knit stitch on right needle. Continue across row, and when row is completed switch needles from right to left and begin again.

Purl Stitch. (see fig. 12). This stitch is actually a knit stitch made backward. Holding needles in same manner as for knitting, insert right needle from above into front of first stitch. (Yarn is guided by right hand and is in front of work.) Loop yarn over needle and pull back through stitch, slipping original stitch off left needle. You now have a purl stitch on your right needle. Continue across row, and when row is completed switch needles from right to left and begin again.

Stockinette Stitch. A combination of alternately knitted and purled rows, this stitch creates work that appears to be all knitting on one side and all purling on the other.

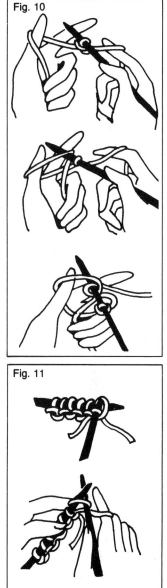

Fig. 10

Fig. 11

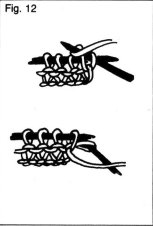

Fig. 12

Garter Stitch. This stitch calls for all rows to be knitted.

Ribbing. Ribbing is created by a combination of knitted and purled stitches in the same row, followed by a row in which the combination is reversed. For example: Row 1—k 2, p 2, k 2, p 2, etc. Row 2—p 2, k 2, p 2, k 2, etc.

Increasing. When instructions direct you to increase, knit a stitch but keep the original stitch on left needle and knit into the back of that stitch. Slip original stitch off left needle. You now have two new stitches on the right needle.

Decreasing. When instructions direct you to decrease at the beginning or middle of a row, simply knit or purl two stitches together. Your decrease will slant to the right. To decrease at the end of a row, slip second to last stitch from left to right needle without knitting or purling. Knit or purl last stitch, pass slipped stitch over last stitch and off needle. This decrease will slant left. (If you are decreasing more than one stitch at the end of a line, count back two stitches for every decrease from last stitch in row.)

Binding off. Knit or purl two stitches, using left needle, slip the first over the second stitch and off needle (see fig. 13). Knit or purl the next stitch and repeat as above until there is one stitch remaining on needle. Break yarn, pass through last stitch, remove stitch from needle and pull yarn until tight. It is important that the binding-off stitches be made loosely so that the work isn't puckered.

Gauge. In order to compare your knitting to the gauge given in a pattern, knit a sample piece of the pattern with the specified yarn and needles. If you knit fewer stitches and rows to the inch, use smaller needles. If you knit more stitches, use larger needles.

Abbreviations. Below are the abbreviations you'll encounter in most knitting patterns. In this book they are sometimes used slightly differently, but the differences are explained as they occur.

* (asterisk)—repeat the instructions that follow the asterisk
beg—beginning or begin
dec(s)—decrease or decreases
inc(s)—increase or increases
k—knit
p—purl
( ) (parentheses)—directions enclosed in parentheses should be repeated
pws—purlwise
sk—skip
sl—slip stitch from left to right needle without knitting or purling
st(s)—stitch or stitches
tbl—through back loop
tog—together
wl bk—wool back
wl fwd—wool forward
work even—continue using the same stitch without increasing or decreasing
yo—form a loop around right needle by winding yarn around it once, knit or purl rest of row and knit or purl loop in next row

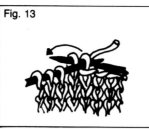

Fig. 13

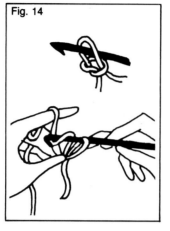

Fig. 14

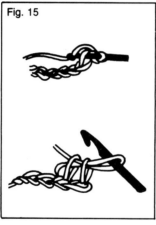

Fig. 15

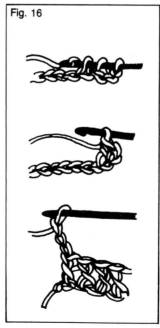

Fig. 16

BLOCKING INSTRUCTIONS FOR KNITTING AND CROCHETING

Place work face down on a padded surface (such as an ironing board) and with rustproof pins pin to correct size, using measurements given in pattern. (Place pins at ¼" intervals.) Cover work with a damp terrycloth towel or pressing cloth and with steam iron press *very lightly.* Do not press down on iron or push iron over surface. Do not press ribbing or raised surfaces. Leave work in position until dry.

SEAMING INSTRUCTIONS

There are two methods given here for joining seams of knitted or crocheted items, backstitching and weaving. To backstitch a seam, pin pieces to be seamed right sides together and sew seam with backstitch, using a needle threaded with the same yarn as was used to make the garment. Don't pull yarn too tightly or seams will pucker. To weave a seam, place pieces right side up with edges to be joined touching. Using a needle threaded with the same yarn as was used to make the garment, bring needle up through the end stitch in top row of left-hand piece and insert it in corresponding stitch on right. Carry yarn under one row on wrong side and bring needle up through the end stitch of third row on right side. Insert needle in corresponding stitch on left side, carry yarn under one row on wrong side and bring needle up through end stitch of fifth row on left side. Repeat until seam is joined.

CROCHETING GLOSSARY

Chain Stitch. The chain stitch is the foundation of your work. To start this stitch, make a slip knot near the end of the yarn and slip loop over hook. Close up loop by pulling yarn attached to ball until loop is snug around hook. Hold hook in right hand (see fig. 14) as you would a pencil. Loop yarn attached to ball around forefinger of left hand and hold the knot with the thumb and middle finger of left hand. Move hook under yarn (this will be referred to as "yarn over" from now on) and pull loop of yarn through loop on hook. Repeat until you have as many stitches as pattern requires. Practice this stitch until you can make a chain of even stitches.

Single Crochet. Begin this stitch by inserting hook from front under the two upper strands of the second stitch from hook as shown in fig. 15. Yarn over and draw yarn through stitch. Yarn over again and draw yarn through the two stitches that are on the hook. Continue as above in next stitch and across row. Make one chain stitch at end of row and turn. Make the next row in the same way.

Double Crochet. Yarn over hook and insert hook from front under two upper strands of fourth stitch from hook. Yarn over and draw yarn through two loops on hook. (See fig. 16.) Two loops still remain. Yarn over and draw through both loops. One loop remains on hook and one double crochet is made. Repeat in next stitch and across row. Make three chain stitches at end of row, turn work and begin first double crochet of this row in the second double crochet of the preceding row.

Half Double Crochet. Yarn over hook and insert hook from front under the two upper strands of third stitch from hook. (See fig. 17.) Yarn over hook and draw yarn through stitch. Yarn over hook and draw through the three loops on hook. Repeat in next stitch and across row. Make two chain stitches at end of row and turn work.

Treble Crochet. Yarn over hook two times and insert hook from front under two upper strands of fifth stitch from hook (see fig 18). Yarn over and draw yarn through stitch. Yarn over and draw yarn through two of the four loops on hook. Yarn over and draw through two of the three loops on hook. Yarn over and draw through the two loops on hook. Repeat in next stitch and across row. Make four chain stitches at end of row and turn.

Slip Stitch. This stitch is used to form a circle (as is done in the Crochet Rose in Scentsations). Insert hook from front under the two upper strands of chain stitch. Yarn over hook, draw yarn through both stitch and loop on hook.

Gauge. Make a 3″ square of pattern stitches using the yarn and needles called for by instructions. Place pattern swatch flat and mark off a 1″ or 2″ square in center of swatch with pins. Count stitches and rows and compare with gauge given in pattern. If you have the same number, you are crocheting to the same gauge as pattern. If you have more stitches and rows, you are crocheting too tightly and should use a larger hook. If you have fewer stitches or rows, you are crocketing too loosely and should use a smaller hook.

See Knitting Glossary for blocking and seaming instructions.

Abbreviations. Below are the abbreviations you'll encounter in most crocheting patterns. In this book they are sometimes used slightly differently, but the differences are explained as they occur.
*(asterisk)—repeat the instructions that follow the asterisk
beg—beginning
ch—chain
dc—double crochet
dec(s)—decrease or decreases
hdc—half double crochet
inc(s)—increase or increases
lp(s)—loop or loops
( ) (parentheses)—directions enclosed in parentheses should be repeated
pat—pattern
rnd—round
sc—single crochet
sk—skip
sl st—slip stitch
sp(s)—spaces
st(s)—stitch or stitches
tr—treble crochet
yo—yarn over

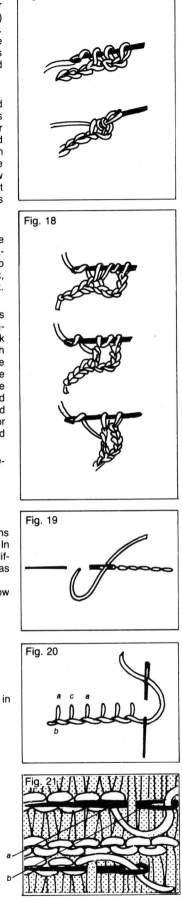

Fig. 17

Fig. 18

Fig. 19

Fig. 20

Fig. 21

Backstitch. Bring needle up and down through fabric to make one straight stitch (see fig. 19); on underside of fabric make another straight stitch. Reverse sewing direction and insert needle at the end of the first stitch. Continue in the same manner, making sure that all the stitches are of the same length.

Blanket Stitch (open). Work from left to right and think of yourself as working between two horizontal lines (see fig. 20). Bring needle up through fabric on the lower line and insert needle on upper line at *a*, leaving thread loose. Bring needle up through fabric on lower line at *b*, over the loose thread and through loop of the first stitch. Insert needle in the top line at *c* and continue across.

Cable Stitch (for smocking) (see fig. 21). Working from left to right, bring needle up on the left side of the leftmost tuck at *a*, bring thread over tuck, insert needle at *b* through tuck, emerging close to *a* (thread should be under needle). Repeat the same procedure at the next tuck, but this time the thread should be over needle. Repeat across, alternating thread position.

Chain Stitch. Begin this stitch (see fig. 22) by bringing needle up through fabric to right side. With thumb, hold thread to one side, insert needle as close as possible to where thread came up through fabric. Take a short stitch on wrong side of fabric and bring up needle through fabric and thread loop to form chain. It is important that the stitches on the wrong side be of uniform size so that the chain will appear even.

Cross-stitch. This old favorite (see fig. 23) is very easy to do. The only trick is to keep the stitches evenly spaced and the same size. Begin by making a row of diagonal stitches from left to right. Finish the stitch by coming back from right to left and crossing the original stitches with stitches on the opposite diagonal.

Diamond Stitch (for smocking; see fig. 24). Working from left to right, bring needle up through fabric and pick up a few threads with a stitch in the first tuck. Moving in a straight line, take a tiny stitch in the next tuck. Bring needle up about ¼″ from the stitching line and take a tiny stitch in the third tuck. Bring needle back to stitching line and take a tiny stitch in the fourth tuck. Work across. Follow the same procedure for the next line but bring needle *down* ¼″ from stitching line on the tucks that you had stitched ¼″ above stitching line in preceding row, forming diamond shapes.

Feather Stitch (see fig. 25). Working vertically from the top, bring needle up through fabric to right side at *a*. Insert needle at *b* below and to the right of the point where the thread emerged while holding the thread that extends from *a* to *b* to the left with thumb. Bring needle up through fabric at *c*, between *a* and *b*, and over thread. Insert needle at *d* below and to the left of *a*, holding thread as you did before but to the right. Bring needle up at *e* midway between *d* and *c* and over thread. Continue as before.

French Knot (see fig. 26). Bring needle up through fabric, wrap the thread around point of needle two or three times and insert needle very close to the place where it emerged and pull tight.

153

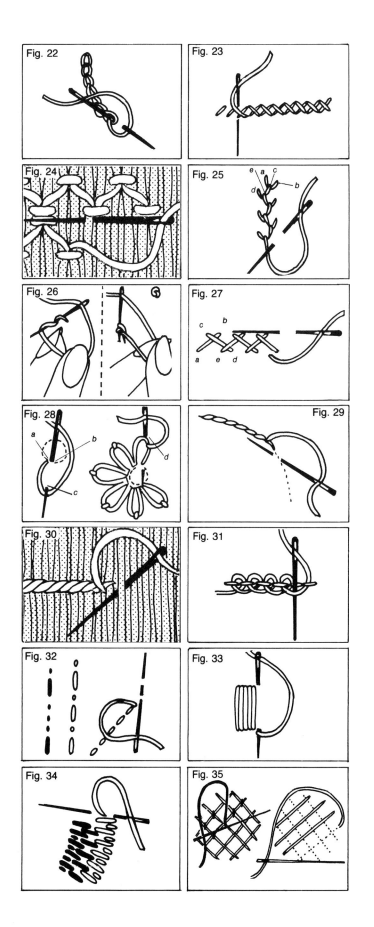

Herringbone or Catch Stitch (see fig. 27). Work left to right and think of yourself as working between two horizontal lines. Bring needle up at *a* through fabric on lower line, insert needle at *b* on upper line and bring needle up at *c* through fabric on upper line. Insert needle at *d* to right on lower line, bring needle up at *e* through fabric and continue across.

Lazy Daisy. The flower stitch (see fig. 28) is very easy to make. Mark a small circle for the center of your flower and bring needle up through edge of this circle at *a*. Form a loop of thread for a petal (hold with thumb) and insert needle a bit to the right of where the thread emerged at *b*. Bring needle out at *c*, take a tiny stitch over loop and insert needle at *d*. Continue making petal loops until flower is completed. For a perfectly symmetrical flower, mark petal tip placement with straight pins.

Outline Stitch. This stitch (see fig. 29) is quite similar to the backstitch. Follow the instructions for backstitch but, when reversing the direction of the stitch, insert needle slightly to the left of the first stitch so that the two overlap a bit.

Outline Stitch (for smocking). A very simple stitch (see fig. 30), this smocking stitch is made by taking a tiny stitch in each tuck, working from left to right.

Pekingese Stitch. This is a very pretty stitch (see fig. 31) used to decorate borders. Make a line of backstitching and then, working left to right, lace through stitches without going through fabric.

Running Stitch. This stitch (see fig. 32) is the one most sewers start with. Just make a series of stitches, long, short, medium, or of varied lengths.

Satin Stitch. One of the basic stitches (see fig. 33), the satin stitch is just vertical or horizontal stitches sewn side by side as closely as possible.

Satin stitch (short and long). The outside rows of this stitch (see fig. 34) are composed of alternating short and long stitches, and the middle rows are composed of stitches of the same length.

Trellis Stitch or Laid Work. Used for crewel embroidery, this stitch is useful for filling in large areas. Fill in entire area with satin stitch (see fig. 35). Starting at shape's widest part bring needle up at *a*, insert at *b*, thus placing a thread diagonally across satin stitches. About ¼″ from *b* bring needle up at *c* and insert at *d*, forming a stitch parallel to the first stitch. Continue until entire shape is covered in this way. Use the same method to make stitches that cross those stitches just made, forming diamond shapes. Hold crossing threads in place by making small stitches at each stitch intersection.

1. *Any good needlecraft shop, department store or from the following mail-order sources:*

Selma's Art Needlework   (212) 722–6469
1645 Second Avenue
New York, New York 10028

Quickit   (212) 759–6470
231 East 53rd Street
New York, New York 10022

Bell Yarn   (212) 674–1030
10 Box Street
Brooklyn, New York 11222

Yarn Center   (212) 532–2145
868 Sixth Avenue
New York, New York 10001

Coulter Studio   (212) 421–8085
118 East 59th Street
New York, New York 10022

2. *Any good art-supply or hobby shop or from the following mail-order sources:*

Arthur Brown   (212) 575-5555
2 West 46th Street
New York, New York 10036

Sam Flax   (212) 889-2666
25 East 28th Street
New York, New York 10016

3. *Any good hobby shop or from the following mail-order source:*

Allcraft   (516) 433-1660
100 Frank Road
Hicksville, New York 11801

4. *Any good hobby shop or from the following mail-order source:*

Albert Constantine and
Son, Inc.   (212) 792-1600
2050 Eastchester Road
Bronx, New York 10461

5. *Any good hobby shop or from the following mail-order sources:*

Tandy   (212) 947-2533
330 Fifth Avenue
New York, New York 10001

Mac Leather Co.   (212) 964-0850
(Leather only)
424 Broome Street
New York, New York 10013

6. *Any good hobby shop or from the following mail-order source:*

Derby Lane Shell Center   (813) 576-1131
10515 Gandy Boulevard
St. Petersburg, Florida

7. *Most dime stores or from the following mail-order source:*

Wilton Enterprises, Inc.   (312) 785-1144
833 West 115th Street
Chicago, Illinois 60643

8. *Any good hobby or art store or from the following mail-order source:*

McKay Chemical Co.   (212) 783-4340
880 Pacific Street
Brooklyn, New York 11238

9. *Large department stores, hobby shops or from the following mail-order source:*

Caswell-Massey   (212) 675-2210
320 West 13th Street
New York, New York 10014

10. *Department stores, fabric shops or from the following mail-order sources:*

Fabrications   (212) 371-3370
246 East 58th Street
New York, New York 10022

Regents   (212) 355-2039
122 East 59th Street
New York, New York 10022

11. *Hobby shops or from the following mail-order sources:*

Mail Order Plastic   (212) 266-7308
56 Lispenard Street
New York, New York 10013

Industrial Plastic Supply   (212) 226-2010
324 Canal Street
New York, New York 10013

12. *Hobby shops, art-supply stores or the following mail-order source:*

S. A. Bendheim   (212) 226-6370
122 Hudson Street
New York, New York 10013

13. *Large department stores, needlecraft shops or the following mail-order source:*

Rug Crafters   (415) 332-1070
Village Fair
777 Bridgeway
Sausalito, California 94965

14. *Fabric shops, department stores or the following mail-order source:*

Central-Shippee   (212) 243-5415
24 West 25th Street
New York, New York 10010

15. *Hobby shops or the following mail-order source:*

Magnus Craft Materials   (201) 945-8866
304-8 Cliff Lane
Cliffside Park, New Jersey 07010

16. *Plumbing supply stores or the following mail-order source:*

New York Plumber Specialty
Company   (212) 665-2500
20 Bruckner Boulevard
Bronx, New York 10454

17. *Dime stores*

18. *Department stores*

19. *Hobby shops*

20. *Art-supply stores*

21. *Hardware stores*

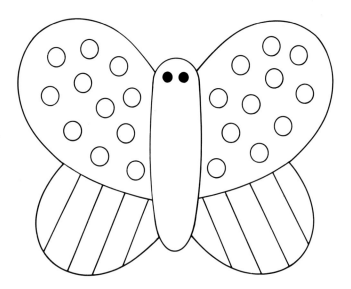

FAT COOKIES

enlarge twice
enlarging instructions are on page 150

HAPPY BIRTHDAY!

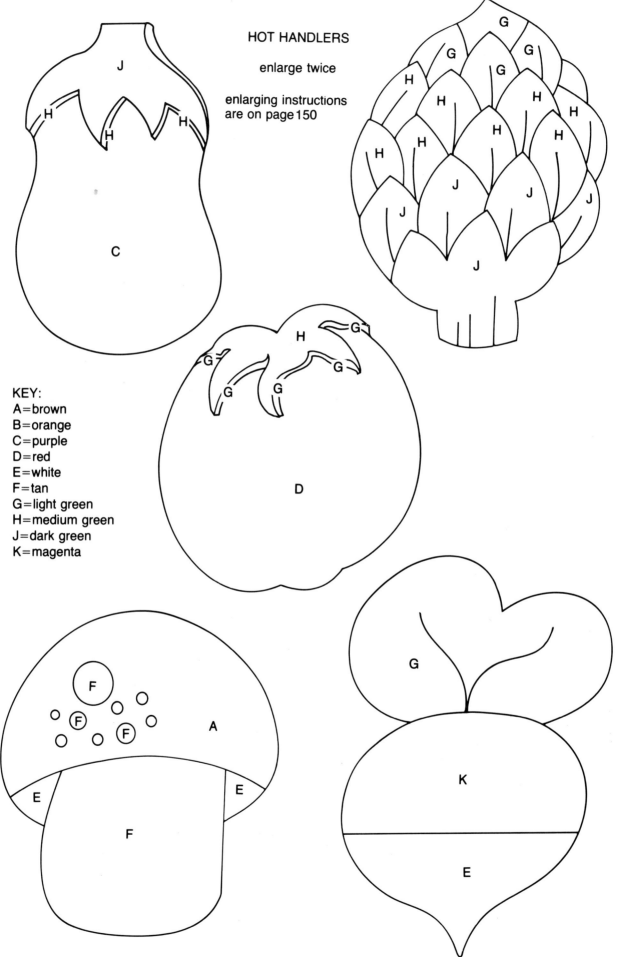

HOT HANDLERS

enlarge twice

enlarging instructions
are on page 150

KEY:
A=brown
B=orange
C=purple
D=red
E=white
F=tan
G=light green
H=medium green
J=dark green
K=magenta

PARTY PINAFORE

NOTE: This is not a layout guide. Pin all pattern pieces to fabric before cutting. Seam allowance of ⅝″ given.

1 square=1 inch

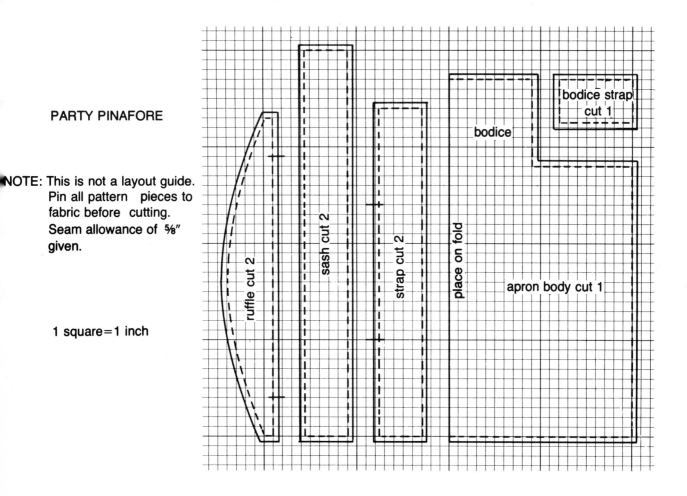

BARGELLO RUG

10 rows C, 6 rows A, 3 rows B, 10 rows C, 3 rows D, 10 rows C, 5 rows E, 7 rows F, inset 1, 7 rows F, 5 rows E, 10 rows C, 3 rows H, 10 rows C, 5 rows F, 3 rows H, inset 2, 3 rows E, 10 rows C, 5 rows G, 7 rows D, inset 3, 7 rows D, 5 rows G, 10 rows C, 3 rows F, 10 rows C, 3 rows B, 7 rows A, 10 rows C

KEY: A=red, B=white, C=black, D=turquoise, E=green, F=yellow, G=orange, H=magenta

1 square = 1 inch

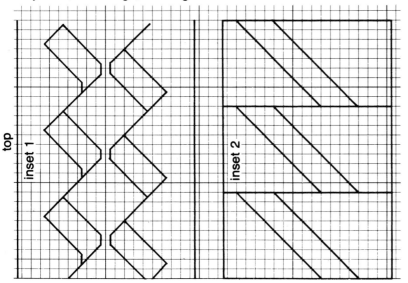

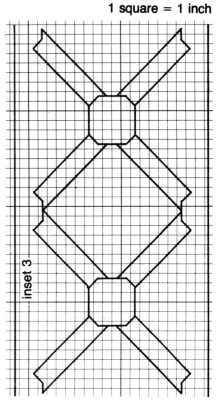

159

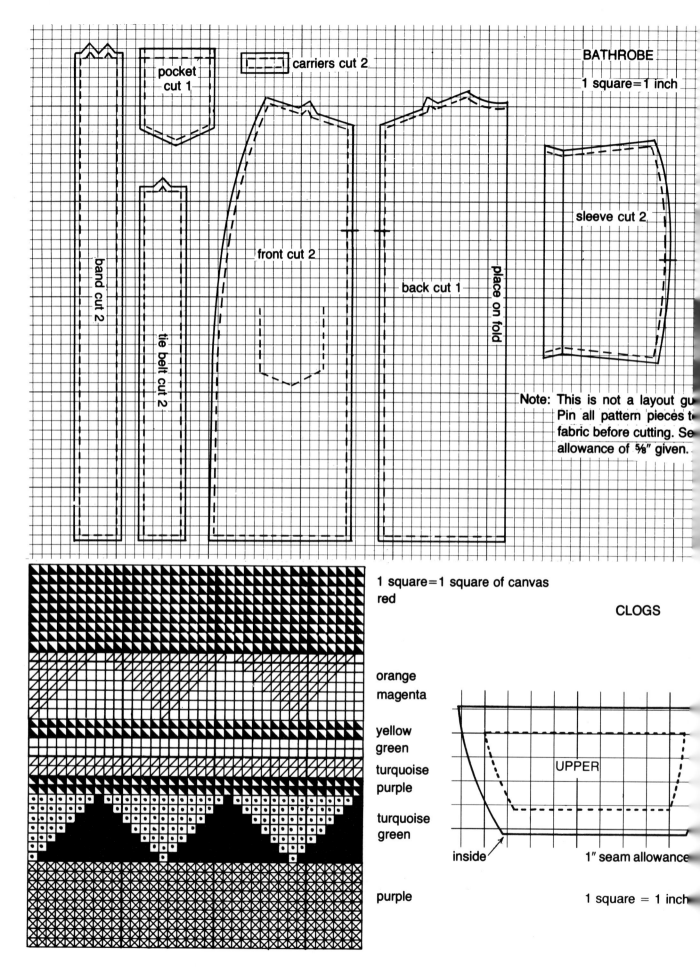

pocket cut 1

carriers cut 2

BATHROBE

1 square=1 inch

sleeve cut 2

band cut 2

tie belt cut 2

front cut 2

back cut 1

place on fold

Note: This is not a layout gu
Pin all pattern pieces t
fabric before cutting. Se
allowance of ⅝" given.

1 square=1 square of canvas
red

orange
magenta

yellow
green

turquoise
purple

turquoise
green

purple

CLOGS

UPPER

inside

1" seam allowance

1 square = 1 inch

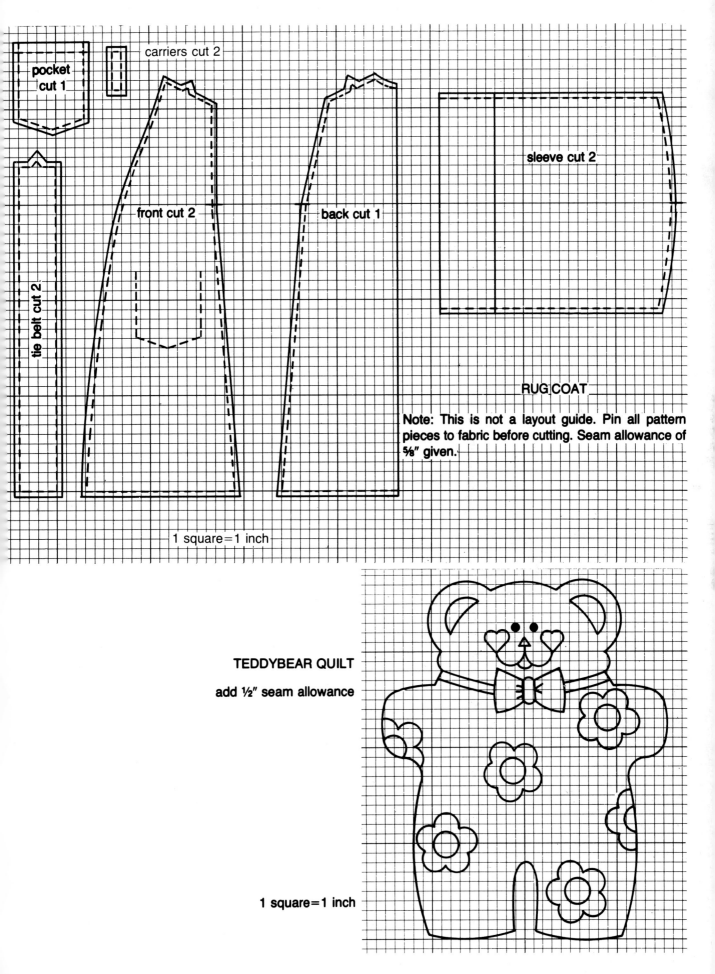

pocket
cut 1

carriers cut 2

tie belt cut 2

front cut 2

back cut 1

sleeve cut 2

RUG COAT

Note: This is not a layout guide. Pin all pattern pieces to fabric before cutting. Seam allowance of ⅝" given.

1 square=1 inch

TEDDYBEAR QUILT

add ½" seam allowance

1 square=1 inch

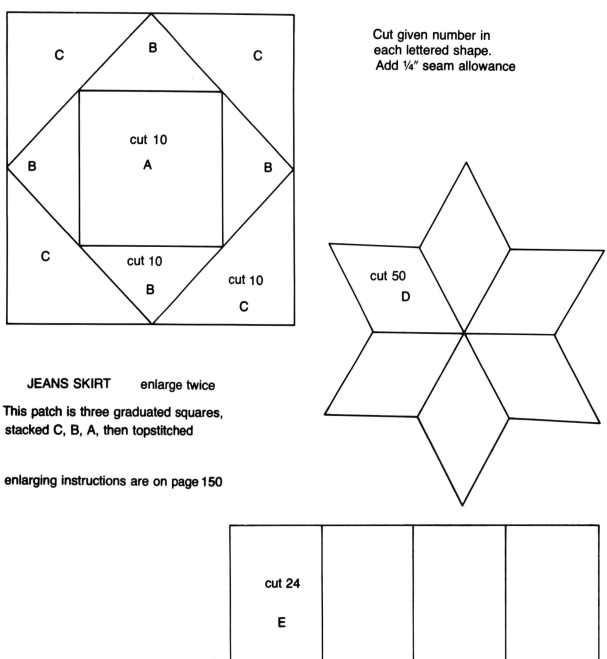

Cut given number in
each lettered shape.
Add ¼" seam allowance

C

B

C

cut 10

A

B

B

C

cut 10

B

cut 10

C

cut 50

D

JEANS SKIRT   enlarge twice

This patch is three graduated squares,
stacked C, B, A, then topstitched

enlarging instructions are on page 150

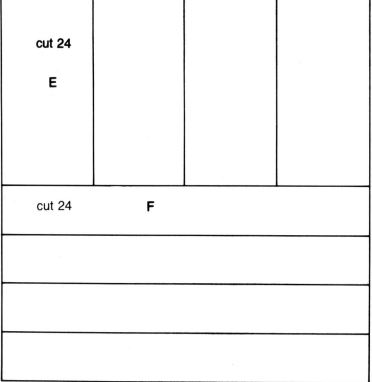

cut 24

E

cut 24   F

continued on next page

APPLIQUÉ TOWELS

enlarge twice,
add ¼″ seam allowance

enlarging instructions
are on page 150

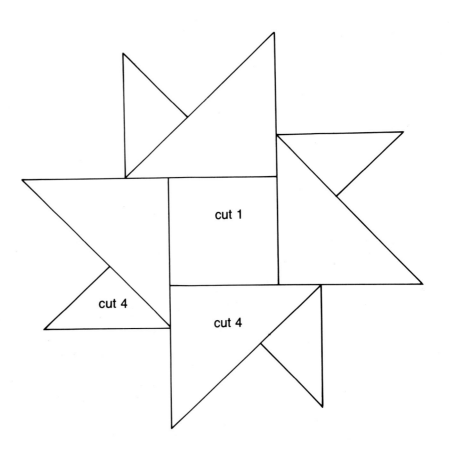

cut 1

cut 4

cut 4

JEANS SKIRT

enlarge twice

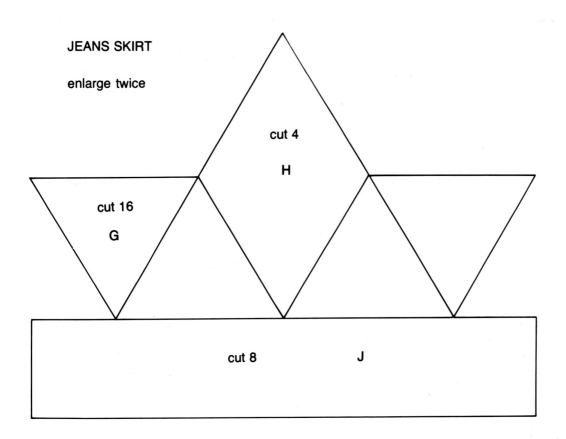

cut 4

H

cut 16

G

cut 8   J

FELT FUN HOUSE

1 square=1 inch
add ¼" seam allowance
where indicated

front façade

back façade

front

side

back

side

continued on next page

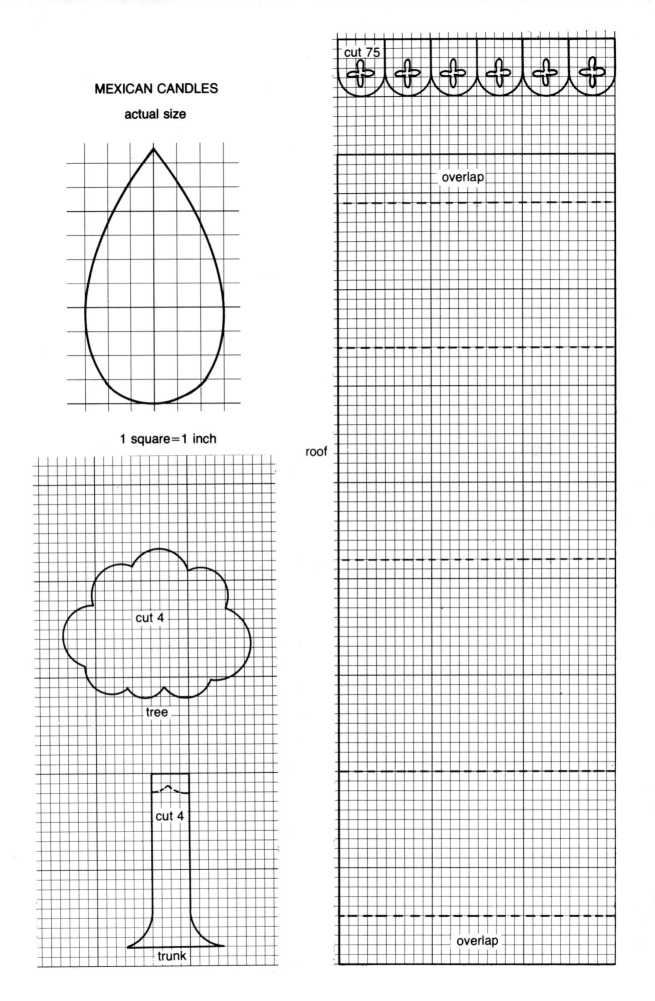

MEXICAN CANDLES

actual size

1 square=1 inch

cut 75

overlap

roof

cut 4

tree

cut 4

trunk

overlap

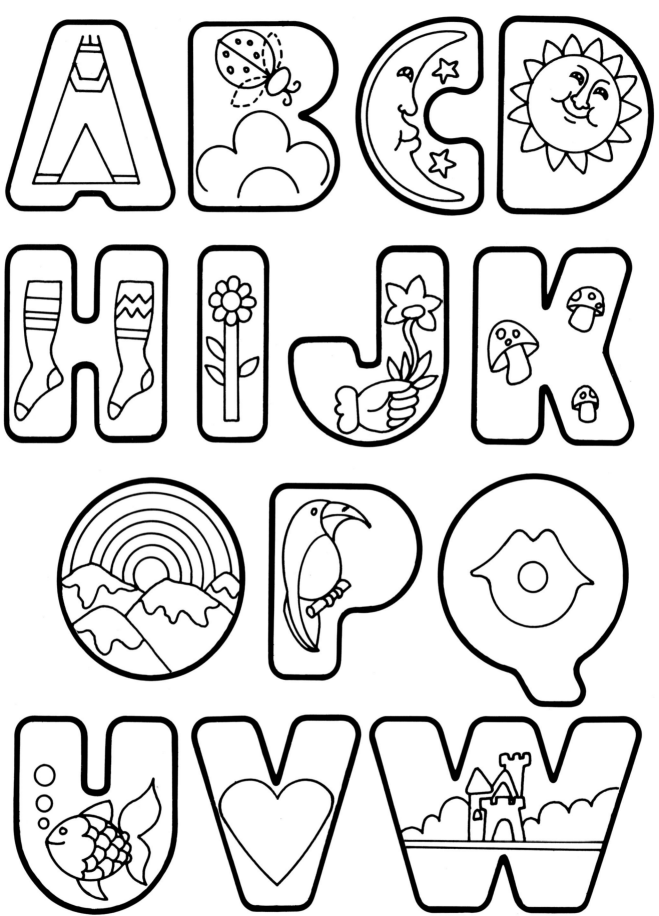

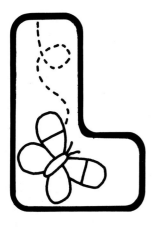

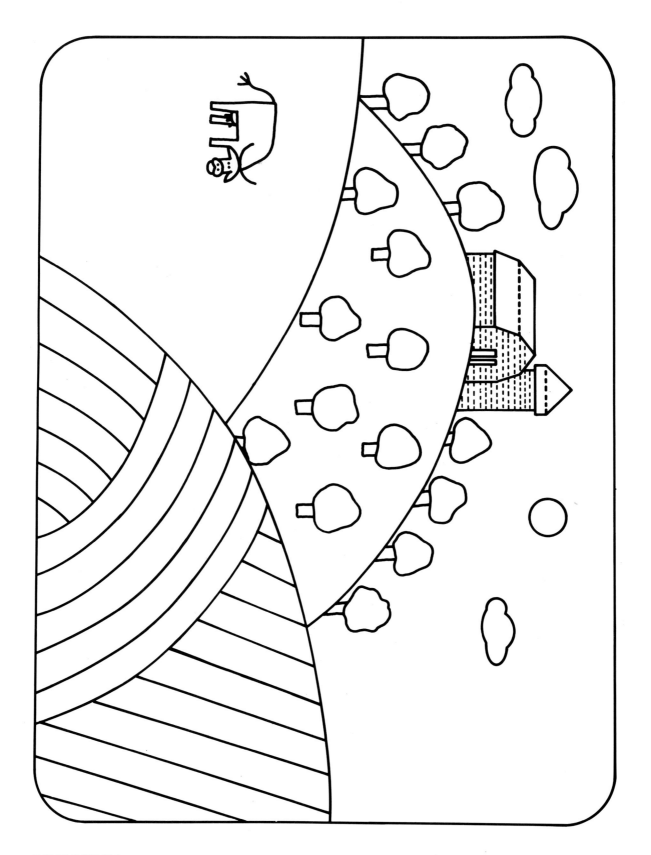

CALICO TRAY

enlarge twice

enlarging instructions are on page 150

continued on next page

CALICO TRAY   enlarge twice

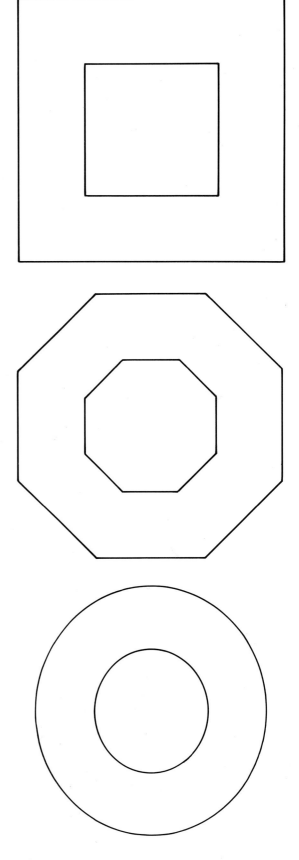

DECO ETCHING   actual size

CLAY FRAMES   enlarge twice

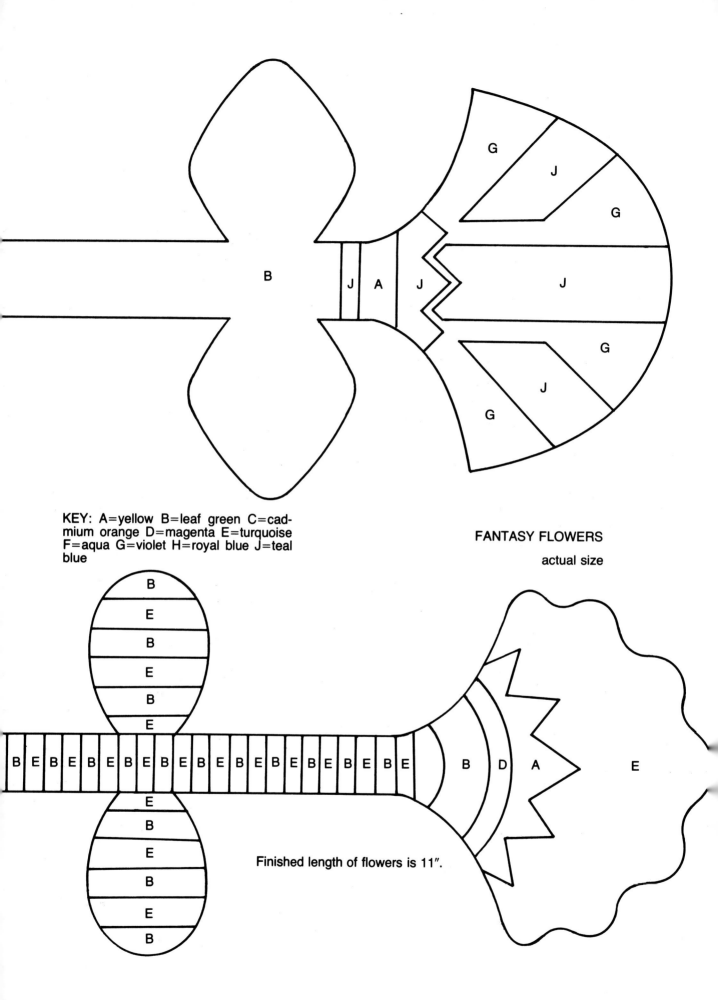

KEY: A=yellow B=leaf green C=cadmium orange D=magenta E=turquoise F=aqua G=violet H=royal blue J=teal blue

FANTASY FLOWERS

actual size

Finished length of flowers is 11".

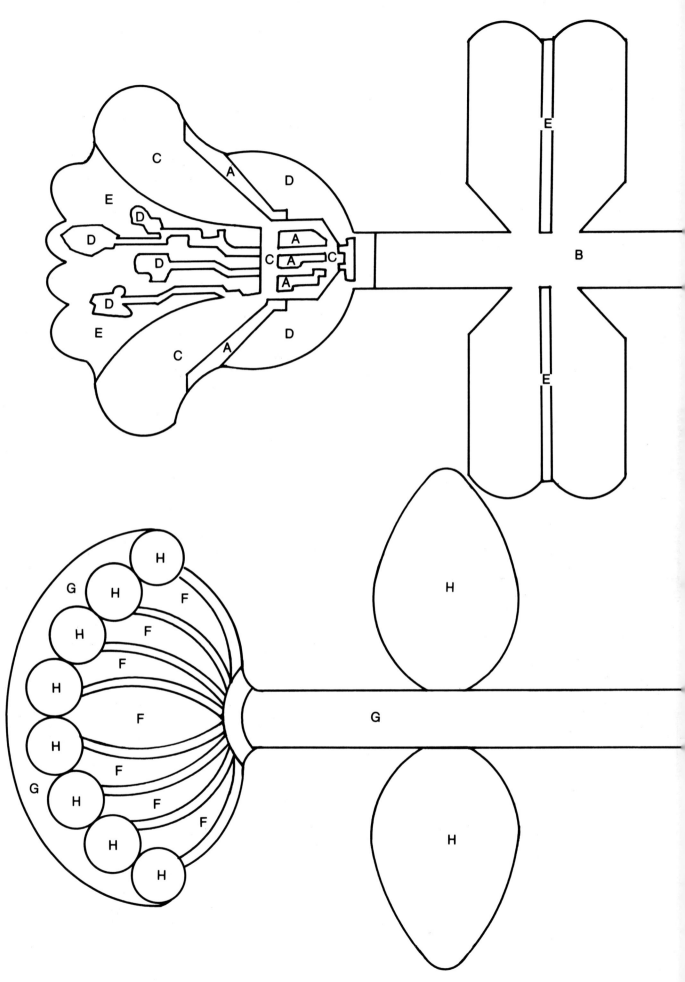

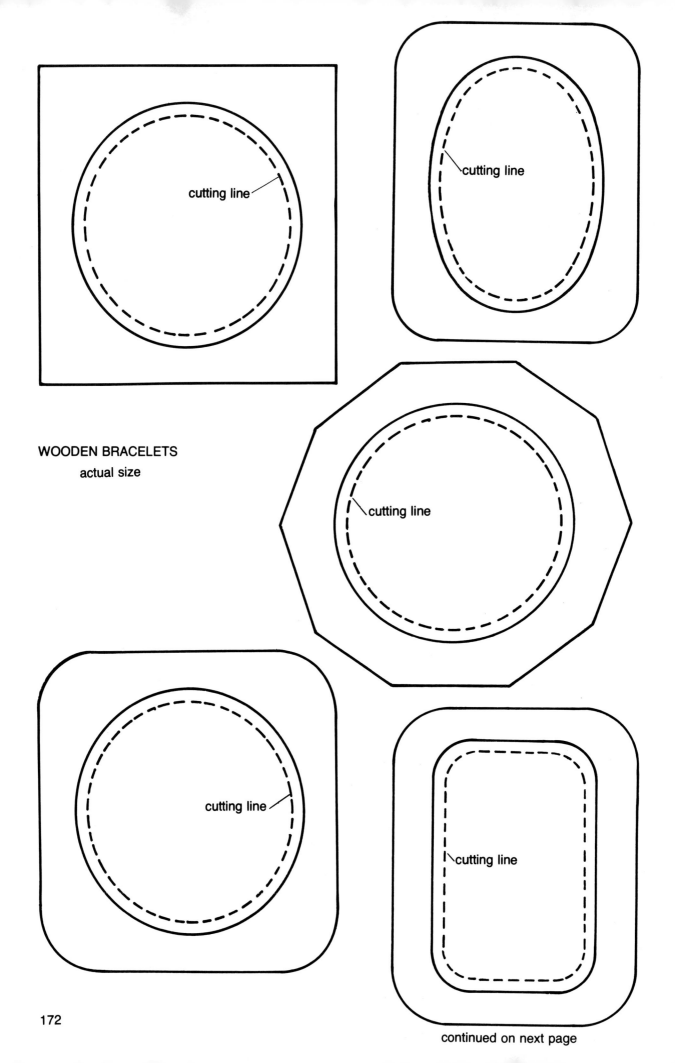

WOODEN BRACELETS
actual size

cutting line

cutting line

cutting line

cutting line

cutting line

continued on next page

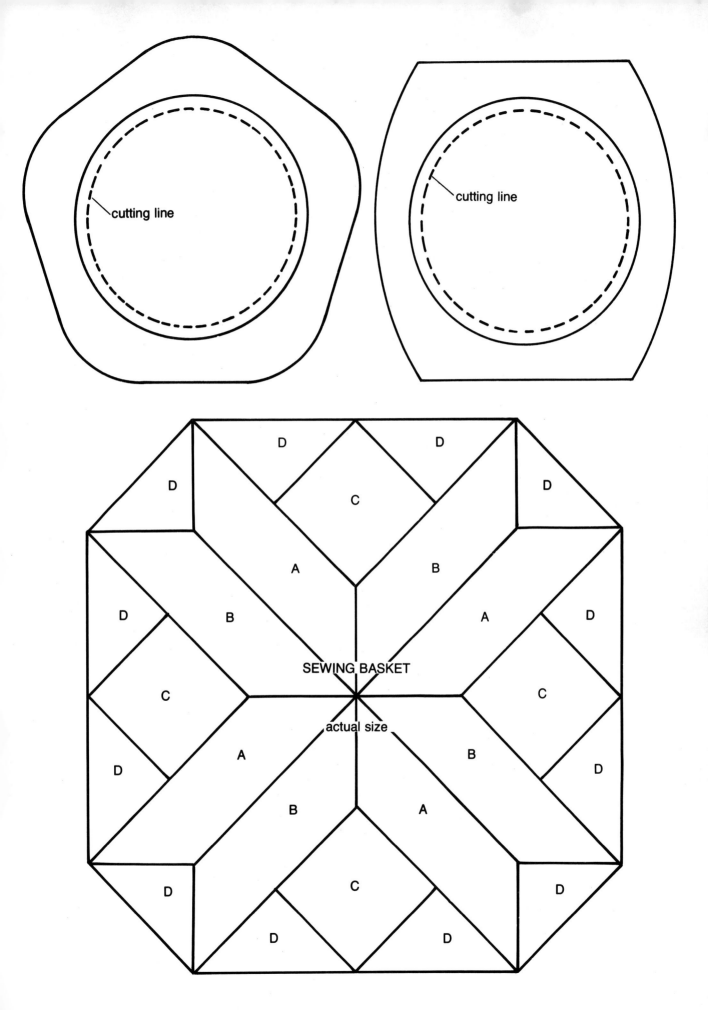

cutting line

cutting line

D D

D D

C

A B

D B A D

SEWING BASKET

C C

actual size

A B

D D

B A

D D

C

D D

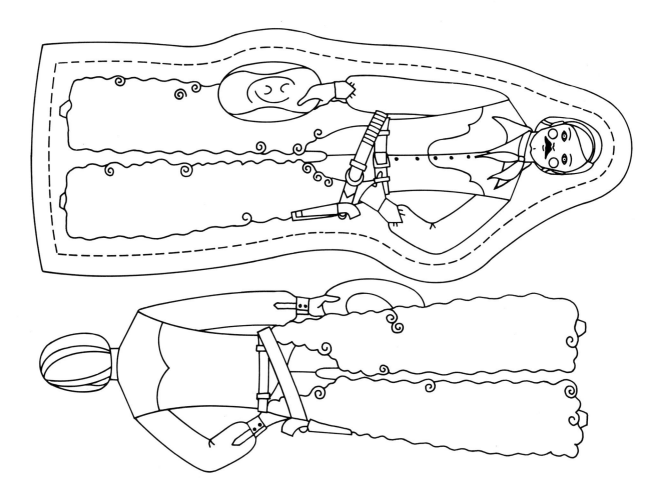

STUFFED DOLLS

enlarge twice

enlarging instructions are on page 150

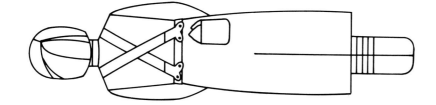

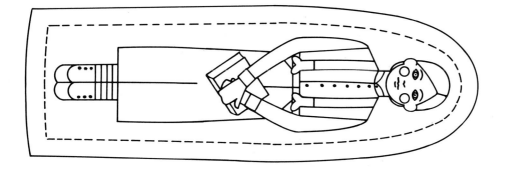

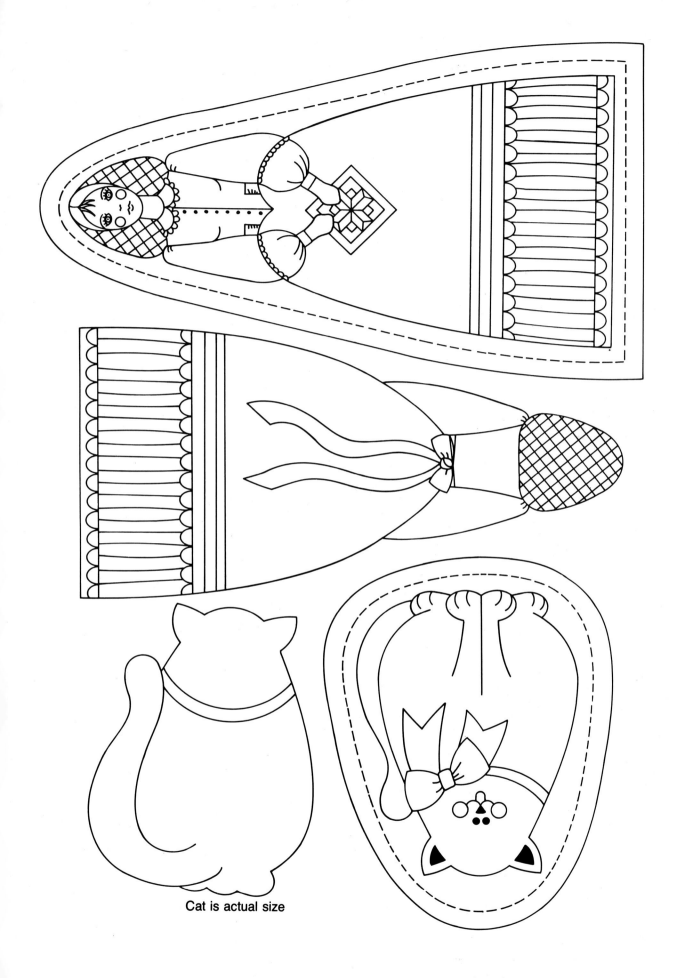

Cat is actual size

continued on next page

175

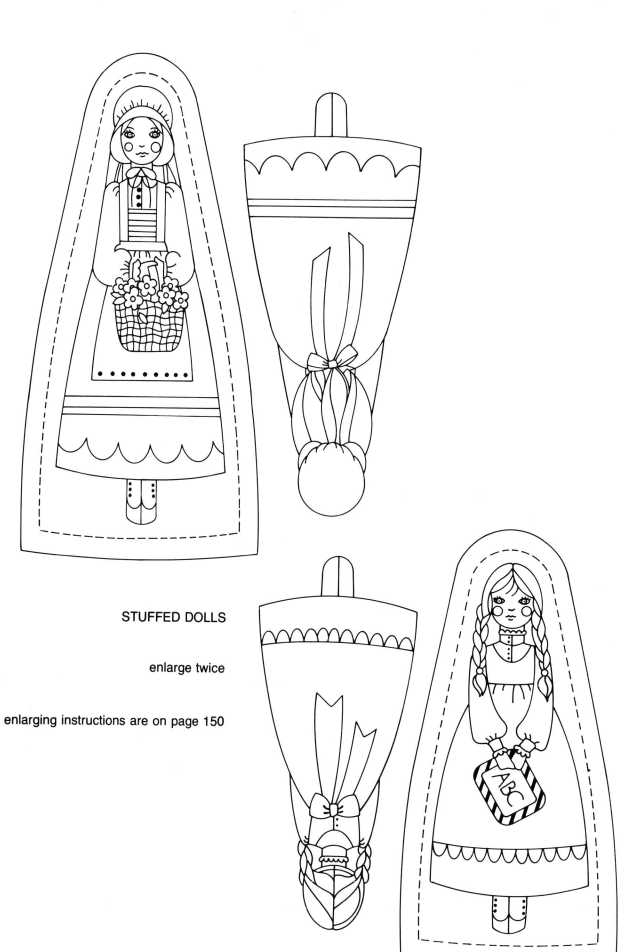

STUFFED DOLLS

enlarge twice

enlarging instructions are on page 150

SCENTSATIONS

actual size

cut two of each

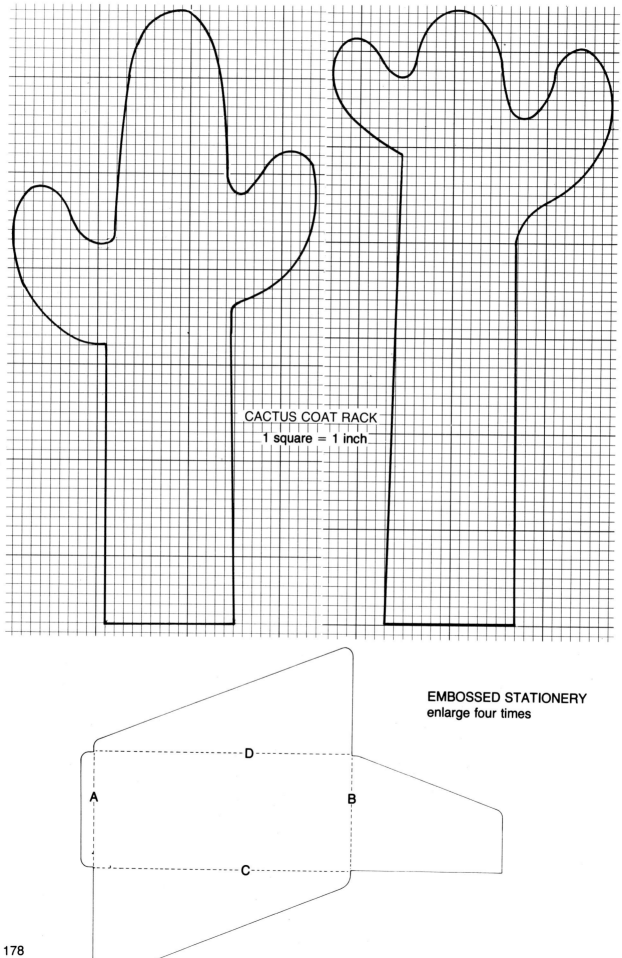

CACTUS COAT RACK
1 square = 1 inch

EMBOSSED STATIONERY
enlarge four times

D

A

B

C

BATH RUG

enlarge four times

KEY: A=wheat, B=wine, C=yellow, D=bright green,
E=dark blue, F=medium blue, G=pink, H=rust, J=light
blue

TREE TRIMMERS

actual size